KAREN DALTON

Songs, Poems, and Writings

By: Peter F. Walker

A collection of Songs, Poems and Writings from the reclusive 60's Folk Singer, Jazz Interpreter, and "Song Stylist" Karen Dalton.

Includes the songs that made up her "repertoire" and embodied the music that influenced not only Karen, but other iconic figures of the 60's. A root source for. and best of friends with Tim Hardin, Fred Neil, and Bob Dylan, as well as many other lesser known musicians. Karen left her mark on the "folk music movement" and is today celebrated as "the white Billie Holiday". Her re-discovery has prompted world wide interest. Despite her reclusive nature, Karen left a rich legacy of information in her personal collection of songs and writings, reproduced here for the first time.

These are the songs and poems as well as excerpts from her diaries which shed light on and insights into the life and times of this obscure but precious music legend.

Ark Press
PO Box 584
Woodstock, NY
12498
ISBN: 978-1-939374-00-4
E-Mail Karendaltonsongsandpoems@yahoo.com
Facebook: Karen Dalton Songs, Poems and Writings

CONTENTS

BIOGRAPHY

The usual dates and places are available on line, as is the discography.

All – Music Guide has a nice article about Karen and has a complete list of her recorded works.

biography

by Richie Unterberger – All Music Guide

"A cult singer, 12-string guitarist, and banjo player of the New York 1960s folk revival, Karen Dalton still remains known to very few, despite counting the likes of Bob Dylan and Fred Neil among her acquaintances. This was partly because she seldom recorded, only making one album in the 1960s -- and that didn't come out until 1969, although she had been known on the Greenwich Village circuit since the beginning of the decade. It was also partly because, unlike other folksingers of the era, she was an interpreter who did not record original material. And it was also because her voice -- often compared toBillie Holiday, but with a rural twang -- was too strange and inaccessible to pop audiences. Nik Venet, producer of her debut album, went as far as to remark in Goldmine, "She was very much like Billie Holiday. Let me say this, she wasn't Billie Holiday but she had that phrasing Holiday had and she was a remarkable one-of-a-kind type of thing.... Unfortunately, it's an acquired taste, you really have to look for the music."

Dalton grew up in Oklahoma, moving to New York around 1960. Peter Stampfel of the Holy Modal Rounders, who was in her backup band in the early '70s, points out in his liner notes to the CD reissue of her first album that "she was the only folk singer I ever met with an authentic 'folk' background. She came to the folk music scene under her own steam, as opposed to being 'discovered' and introduced to it by people already involved in it." There is a photograph from February 1961 (now printed on the back cover of the It's So Hard to Tell Who's Going to Love You the Best reissue) of Dalton singing and playing with Fred Neil and Bob Dylan, the latter of whom was barely known at the time. Unlike her friends she was unable to even capture a recording contract, spending much of the next few years roaming around North America.

Dalton was not comfortable in the studio, and her Capitol album It's So Hard to Tell Who's Going to Love You the Best came about when Nik Venet, who had tried unsuccessfully to record her several times, invited her to a Fred Neil session. He asked her to cut a Neil composition, "Little Bit of Rain," as a personal favor so he could have it in his private collection; that led to an entire album, recorded in one session, most of the tracks done in one take. Dalton recorded one more album in the early '70s, produced by Harvey Brooks (who had played on some '60sDylan sessions). Done in Bearsville Studios in Woodstock, it, like her debut, had an eclectic assortment of traditional folk tunes, blues, covers of soul hits ("When a Man Loves a Woman," "How Sweet It Is"), and contemporary numbers by singer/songwriters (Dino Valente, the Band's\ Richard Manuel). the Band's "Katie's Been Gone," included on The Basement Tapes, is rumored to be about Dalton."

_--

Defining a friendship, or someone else s life, is entirely subjective. I can only relate what I saw and know from my point of view.

I know nothing about Karen's life growing up in Enid, Oklahoma except that she was collecting music lyrics and songs from an early age, and that music was the focus of her life.   Her mother, Mrs Evelyn Carter, was quoted as saying "Karen could play any instrument she wanted to including a violin I once gave her. She taught herself how to sight sing classical music or any other kind." When she was fourteen years old the family Doctor told them that "She's a real artist."   Karen's talent was unique and obvious even then.

I also don't know anything about her family life, except for her relationship with her son Johnny-Lee Murray.

Johhny-Lee was around during the last years of his mothers life and we got to spend some time together. I heard him sing a couple times and am convinced he has inherited his mothers talent. I hope at some point in his life he will decide to develop his obvious ability. I would like to hear that.

Despite her own suffering through the many years that she battled the AID's that was wracking her body in a way that drugs never had she never lost her cheerful spirit and sweet demeanor. It made her appear fragile as a wisp, nevertheless she commuted to NY, worked at low pay jobs, and struggled to stay alive.

Karen was born in 1937, a year before me. She died in 1993.
I met Her in 1961. She was twenty four years old

In the fall of 1961 I was visiting Singer-Songwriter John Morier in his apartment in Cambridge. John had recently married a Cambridge girl, Lynn Decker. The happy couple were regulars on the all night music scene that was flourishing in Boston/Cambridge at the time.

We were swapping songs and guitar licks when the door opened
Karen Dalton and
Richard Tucker swooped in like a breath of fresh air. Reality on the hoof.
In a world and scene of amateurs, semi-pros and wannabe's Karen and Richard were the real McCoy. Terrific quality instruments, slick New York cool casual clothes, and an air of confidence and nobility. They knew who they were. They were on a mission.

They unpacked their guitars and Banjo's and began singing the most authentic and heartfelt folk material most of us had ever heard. It was only many years later I realized that she had been collecting her material since childhood in Oklahoma. She was one of the most authentic root sources of material for the folk music movement. At the time she appeared, quick, competent, and full of purpose as she brought her artistic talents to bear on the political issues of the time.

It was the beginning of the 60's and people were looking around for a genuine American heritage in a fast emerging post war plastic world. Television was dumbing down America, and authentic root folk sources like Sonny Terry, Blind Lemon, Leadbelly, Billie holiday, Doc Watson, Odetta, and Karen Dalton were the last remnants of a different era. The last of the old time singers from a world of oral tradition which predated both radio and television were giving way to a new generation of musicians.

The new generation inspired by the songs of the deep south, dust bowl and union activists, expanding pioneers, and the poor and poignant were creating a new movement of social protest. The joy, and suffering, story's and folklore of the music from many diverse cultures and parts of the world was fusing into a American folk music that expressing the feelings and spirit of a nation, in all of its myriad forms and colors.

It was a great evening and in the wee hours, helping them load their magnificent instruments into their spiffy car, I remember thinking, that these people were real professionals, dedicated totally on every level to their craft, and working at their profession like a trial lawyer, or a brain surgeon works at their's.

I don't remember seeing Richard after that, but shortly after Tim Hardin showed up on the scene, followed a few months later by regular visits by the Holy Modal Rounders. (Peter Stampfel and Steve Weber).

Tim and Karen were close friends, and in 1963 Karen was back on the scene in Cambridge. Back from tours and gigs around the country, but living as a single woman, Often hanging out with Tim. Timmy was coming out with his first album and everybody loved his songs.

Karen would come into the Cambridge Folklore Center on Mount Auburn street in Harvard Square, just a block from the "Club 47". She would browse through the music collection and check out the many great instruments, more often than not, she would contribute a song, or a lyric, or a guitar or banjo lick to the perennial jam going on.

I had left Boston at age 14 (1952) and had traveled, hitchhiking, first to the Grand Old O'pry and then throughout all of the deep south, Texas, the southwest, most of the north west and California.

My interest in folk music and it's roots had led me to establish the "New Scene Folklore Center" in Boston and Cambridge. Karen and I had one particular thing in common. It was an honest and passionate interest in the music that reflected the "American Experience" what that was, and where it came from. It was a genuine curiosity and love affair with the music that defined the USA. Later that musical trail would lead me abroad to follow the origins of the music of Spain through North Africa, to India. Karen stayed on the path of our Blues, Folk, Pop, and Jazz heritage.

As far as the snobby local "Folk Hierarchy" were concerned having her picture on the cover of the Ode Banjo catalog was a credential like playing "Grand Ol Opry". Ode Banjo's were the best, coolest, and most reasonably priced available in the US at the time. And could only by bought directly from the factory, from the catalog.

Talk about obscure and exclusive, among the hard core folkies it forever firmly established her bona fides and made her a celebrity.

Over time we became friends. Karen, Tim, and The Holy Modal rounders actively participated when I produced a 72 hour concert in 1963, raising money for Boston Children's Hospital. The Kennedy family were very helpful and supportive.

Len Chandler flew up from New York City, and was a fireball of education, talent, and wisdom. Besides being a world class super-talent contemporary singer/songwriter he represented the interests of the SNCC, (Student Non-violent Coordinating Committee) which was doing the boots on the ground work, and being the cutting edge of Martin Luther Kings efforts in the Deep South. He asked for the community's support and got it. Karen went on to play for SNCC events.

And so did I a year later by producing a 2'nd 72 hour concert in Boston in Copley Square. This time it was for SNCC. Karen and Tim also played at that one. I remember a heart-rendering rendition by Bobby Nuewirth of "The Halls of Red Wing". One of the most memorable performance of all, in my entire life experience, was done by Taj Majal. He played Louie Louie for nearly 40 of the 72 hours of the concert, and kept the ball rolling in the wee small hours, and early mornings. All in support of SNCC, Dr. King, and the movement. Taj is a true American hero and a great man.

I have a clipping from 1964 featuring Karen Dalton appearing at benefits in support of SNCC, Dr. King, and the movement. She was attending leadership conferences on race and religion. At some point she came in contact with Gwendolyn Gillon the articulate and passionate 18 year old field secretary of SNCC who was speaking out at university's organizing support for the civil rights movement, and Dr King. Gwendolyn was quoited as saying "I'd like to be arrested, because then I'll know even better what its like". It was the spirit of the times. and Karen was a part of it.

I was off traveling to Spain, Africa, Mexico and California and although I saw Tim in Los Angeles about a year later, I didn't see Karen again until NYC around 1967, at Tim's place in NY on the west side. We Saw each other briefly over the next couple of years. She Headlined at the Ash Grove in L.A. in 69 the same night that Linda Ronstadt was at the Troubadour. So I knew she was still "out and about".

Both of us wound up in Woodstock about 1970. From that time on I would see Karen often at Bob Brainen's house up on the Wittenberg Hill on the back side of Ohayo Mountain in Woodstock. Bob Brainen was incredibly intelligent. He Stayed up until nearly dawn and kept several instruments tuned and handy on which he played, wrote sang and shared. His friends affectionately called him "Bobby the Brain".

"The Brain" was one of those people who kept a musical open house. For years whoever was in town would be up there hanging out. Freddy Neil, Tex Koernig, Tim Hardin, Bob Dacey, Becky Brindel, Bruce Gibson, Bob Gibson, and a host of others gathered in the wee hours of the morning to share music, a beer, a bowl, and more music.

From the round table in the kitchen Bob dispensed both wit and wisdom. He often lectured Karen while nurturing her about getting stable and getting her career on track. Bob's good advice and wise council kept many of us together, including both Karen and I during those years of confusion and poverty. He mentored me into my paralegal job with the taxi fleets in the city, and tried hard to get Karen to organize and record a new album. She would try and rally and record, and there were a few tapes, but in the eighties the disease was taking it's toll. And only fragments remain of her efforts.

This went on for years. Woodstock is a small town, less than 3000 people in the winter. At 2 or 3 in the morning, Bob's was the only place to hang out, and network. "have you heard from Freddy??" was a typical question and the latest reports would circulate about the entire far flung social circle of musicians.

During the seventies as winter came on I would often fix up an old truck and build a camper on the back utilizing various designs. "Road testing" often included a trip across country or all over Mexico and back. My contact with Karen was sporadic. When I was around I would stop in wherever she was living and socialize, or most often I would see her up at Bob's.

In the early eighty's I began traveling to Colorado to work the high season in Aspen as a driver for "Mellow Yellow" Taxi Co. For four Winter months I could drive in the blizzards and make enough to finish out the winter in California and come back to Woodstock for the late spring, summer, and fall There were playing jobs available and I could make good money with music, but the driving paid much more, and it was a great chance to socialize with the rich, famous, and powerful. The tips were great. It was the first time I had made money in years. My life started to change.

It was coming back from one of these trips that I stopped up to Bob's place and found Karen on the fold out bed in the living room. "Get the kids out of here" she yelled. Karen had become quite close to my son's and had taken to regularly visiting and taking an interest in them. It was typical of her sweet nature.

"Get the kids out of here" she hollered, "I've got some kind of terrible flu and I don't want them to catch it". She was frail and sweaty, and obviously very ill. It was her first bout with AID's. Through the rest of the 80's she lived with the disease. Most of the time she functioned almost normally, and kept an apartment in the city and a residence in Woodstock.

By the mid eighty's I was commuting to the city for a para-legal job with a huge taxi fleet and often gave her a ride coming or going. I had gone back to school at City College of New York and had gotten a Para-legal certificate. This empowered me to do litigation for the NY taxi fleets under the supervision of a licensed attorney. It also enabled me to send my kids through school, something Karen heartily approved of.

We would ride and talk on the city commutes, mostly about music, often about life. I played enough every day to keep my hands working, but only played a couple benefits a year in those days. Karen always encouraged me to sing and would talk about how to approach a note from below and bring it up to pitch, like a "shruti"in Indian music. (There are over twenty ways to approach a note in Indian music depending on the raga and the scale) I had studied "shrutis with Ali Akbar Khan, so once again we had something in common to relate to.

One time I was complaining about something as we made our regular drive down to the city. Karen said "Peter, why don't you just shut up and enjoy being rich?? I asked her what she meant, I said "I am struggling to pay the bills". Karen said "Peter your rich, look at this car were riding in, (Chevy caprice with 30,000 miles on it) you got a good job, (Taxi Fleet Para-legal) your kids are in a good school (East Manhattan). Your rich, compared to most people." I hadn't thought of it that way at the time but it was true, I was doing well.

Like most things it depended on your point of view. The life style of the eighty's was a big step up for me economically. Especially when viewed from the perspective of someone who had seen me living in the camper trucks with young children and a a tiny wood stove for over a decade prior to then. Associating with the immigrant cab drivers in the city had a positive effect on my work ethic and priorities. Karen saw this and approved. In many ways she was truly "Mama Karen".

Throughout all the years in the many hours that we spent together over those years, that I knew her and that we were friends, from 1961 until her death in 1993, Karen and I never talked about drugs, and never shared any. I knew she had a private life, as did I, and what she did within the rubric of her private world was her business, We each dealt with the pain of our artistic existence in our own way. If I didn't have my kids as a priority, who knows, things might have worked out differently. I had originally been taught that drugs were medicine, and not recreation. Perhaps this viewpoint saved my life in the long run. Perhaps Karen felt the same which would explain her level of functionality. But whatever the perspective, reasoning, or justification, it was not something we discussed or shared. I know that this may come as a surprise to some, and some may not believe it, but it's true. I occasionally saw her with a beer in her hand but never saw any other evidence of alcohol abuse. She struggled with poverty more than any addiction or physical infirmity..

Although sick physically she was fully functional mentally She was a voracious reader and a deep thinker. Her thought processes took her much deeper then her Cherokee philosophy about Mother Earth and Father Sun. It was always apparent that she possessed a special spirituality.

I knew she was struggling to keep her apartment in the Bronx and would make small money passing out fliers and doing other subsistence work. At the end of the week when I would be leaving she would come downtown and be at my apartment ready to go back to Woodstock.
Her diaries express the struggle she faced in the violent neighborhood, with hostile landlords, and ridden with dangerous junkies and thieves. Yet, she had a rent controlled apartment, and it was "her place in the city" I knew how she felt. I'd had a rent controlled apartment in the lower east side in the 60's and it was like owning a home. Her writings are not really diaries in the chronological sense, there are four 5 X 8 diary sized books with writings, poems, songs, comments, insights, and ramblings. The more I read, the more I am impressed.

Like the song collection they are tattered fragments of someone's life that offer a window into the mind and soul.

Here are some excerpts:

> "We construct a subtle contract
>   a parallel conjecture concerning
>   the ultimate conclusions of our confederacy.
>   Our conversations have become a mutual

exercise in concentration and concessions controlled
and conditioned by considerations
of containing and concealing the
consummation of a foregone conclusion
conjures our conversion and conquest
of conformity, consorting and conspiring, consenting and
confessing a confirmation unconsidered
in similar constellations of relations."

"It is apparent to me that the landlord must have some surprise secret tactics. I can see it in the guilty eyes of several of my neighbors. Ben asked to exchange my tenancy for several thousand dollars and to carry out the transaction like the friendly long-time acquaintances we are – (no need for lawyers although he would type out an agreement."

"Lady of contradictions
 Practitioner of spoken fiction
 Satellite of power
 Giving to take and
 Taking with a steal
 Uncanny prayers and brilliant images congeal
 Behind her smile where
 Businessmen take candy
 From Babies"

"What driven need are you faithful before,
 what force steadfast and sirening traces your
 fidelity,, harnesses your deeds
 what powerful entity ignorant and oblivious
 to prayers and supplicants do you worship
 heedless of deity, deed-less and predatory
 precious and specious , special potential
 creating destruct ions, destroying creations
 what leveling gaze what awesome sound
 what hidden idol hovers about your
 dancing, ignoring lewding, careless and

scornful of it's horrendous power, ever
drawing more by it's very disdain and
unbelief to caustic caresses cleaving
ever greater power to it's repertoire
cleaning passion from your breast
craving nothing carrying whatever secret
weights we offer, throwing on contradictions
needless of nourishment, what ultimate
human yoke has found your soul."

" Take advantage of the opportunity to spend time in the country
away from distractions caused by diverse needs. Use the time to
create a new mythology, to recreate a panorama of vision, enlarging,
specifying, painting, pointing out a larger vision then what you lost.
Make it work for yourself. Grab your possibilities and make them
realities."

"Time feeds upon the living".

"What use did addiction serve
Not easing pain, it's not like most often depicted
Get hurt by lover, so get high to ease the pain
Maybe it's so subtly hooking because it's easy to
be devoted, to thrust all that misplaced love, that
spirited charade that captured shadow, to capture
to grab all to myself a mold-able flexible reinforcing
risk you can't risk. Instead of spending lifetimes
learning the song of silence. The descent of desire, one can
short cut, short cut - one can use the frozen food
the instant potatoes the pat passion. One can shout
Death is the universe, the universal equalizer.
Of what import is the color of your skin before
generations of careless colors. One can shout
I wish I could know the hopelessness of shouting,
of any anguished searching, accepting regretting.
One can wish for contemplative peace while
fighting thoughtlessly for a farce that
keeps seeming relative, that insists
on demanding responses – how can meaning
achieve a meaninglessness that says everything?

There is no superhighway, no special bridges
there are many roads but there is distance
and destiny – to think yourself somewhere is
impossible because the action requires caring
enough to go from here to there and the end
is achieved by not caring. The sound of
one hand clapping
If perfect detachment can result in ability
to practice auto kinetic travel-out of body being
and if perfect detachment is achieving
cessation of clinging of desires is a
perfect control of self energy – the super
powers become meaningless once the ways
are available over the means. Enlightenment
precludes not desiring even to be there, not here.
If you knit a sweater for the cold weather
and finish it when the weather is warmer, it's
premise is obsolete. Does possible resumption
of cold weather in future create words beyond
object of strange – beyond poet worth.
If the main worth of creation lies not with the creator
but in expanded energy, time, direction, will used
to create it, what basis for worth is there once it's done?
A shirt for baby finished after the baby's outgrown the size
has worth because of intention, of thought and
planning and eventual conceptual becoming concrete.
Does possibility of using it for another child still
small enough endow finished shirt with worth?
What if there were no future baby's and shirt had
no purpose except pleasing to look at and to touch. Our
need for harmony gives us desire for items with no
utilitarian purpose as such. But the state of mind
engendered through looking at a pleasing creation
is (in a sense) utilitarian (especially to someone seeking
the state of mind it sways). Thus paintings made to
change consciousness . Look at the pattern on this
shirt and develops a feeling of peace, of power
of tenderness etc. Look at this arrangement of
patterns and cure your asthma, and gain tolerance
of wife's irritating ways....

Wow – is that the shadowy developing of man's art and religious art?
How exciting -what a gift to stumble upon.....

I have just discovered a glorious gift – I've
charted where man's religious art (is all
art religious – no some is agnostic) , springs from.
Why art is considered a leisure occupation and why it's not...
In fact – what if outgrown shirt with no use to wear
is used to induce a a calmness and unity
then passing back and forth among tribes
while there is still a need of other clothing
thus creation to satisfy spiritual needs is added
to creating to satisfy body's need.
Perhaps weavers may incorporate psychedelic
designs upon their shirts or blankets."

"yes I believe I can do that with my life
incorporate a special element into this story"

"Has perseverance and fortitude at long last
unfurled the world's ragged banner and
are we finally able to recognize the
propisity of fairy tale time beside
Rocky Mountain, Daylight Saving, and Part.
Do we relent the constant burden of
repentance and ratified aristocracy
walking beside reverberations of our lost world?"

"Richard *** *** *** stole $330 (approximately the amount of my
SSI check) from me March 5th. I was returning $110 to him and
inadvertently showed him the cash belonging to me. He grabbed a
razor blade and held it to my throat demanding all the money
claiming it belonged to him because it had to be the profit I made
from selling $1000 worth of gold he suddenly discovered missing. I
gave him the cash, totally shocked, I ran outside, locking my door
with a padlock, to call the police – While across the street at the
phone I saw him running down the street carrying his coat, I
screamed stop that man he robbed me. Someone grabbed him,.
While waiting for the police he returned all my ID (in front of the

person holding him) and asked to go have breakfast and settle it quietly. He yelled when grabbed that I had stolen from him, his proof was that I was a junkie' The civilian answered why were you running away with your coat and shirt off, - why did you have her ID? Richard kept repeating that he had been robbed. When the police finally came my helper said I can't stay I have a warrant As I went to get them (the police) Richard ran and disappeared when I turned around"

"how much more can a white girl take? My heart is a jack hammer drilling, tearing up pavement – the pavement of peoples lives. Muscles contract trying to contain the pieces. Behind my eyes the throbbing warns...."

One time in 1989 she came to my apartment on The Bowery with deeply blue and blackened hands from from the wrists down. It was dramatic damage. It came from having the circulation cut off from handcuffs. She had been arrested for something related to her job handing out fliers. It was either littering or blocking the sidewalk. The arresting officers had tightened the manacles too much and refused to loosen them for several hours. Eventually her hands recovered. But it was shocking to see what they had done to her. I knew from experience that litigation against the City of New York was among the most difficult types of case to pursue, and didn't try to make a case of it. But I was deeply affected. It was wrong to do that to anyone but especially a musician. The problem was that she had no income, or permanent injuries and thus it was hard to document or claim damages.

Life was not all tragedy and suffering for Karen, she laughed, she hung out, she socialized, she guided other people out of the city and into a healthy country life.

She wrote: " He lives in the light and probable
                    He lives in the might and magical
                    He lives in the highly improbable person "

"Suddenly some hidden, unbidden, heart feeling, health feeding, caring insists on recognition.
Suddenly, shockingly some saving grace crept into my life

crept with all the secrecy of a stamping dinosaur paw, a stomping
elephant walk, an earthshaking soul shining sun stormy
slipping sly and shy sad smiling, sage and simple, sky and soil solid
insistent shouting secret celebrations in suddenly sensible
stubborn action syllables, showing concrete excavations
into a spirit I conjured since memory began
in the night shadows of solitary childhood dreaming
in the magical heroes of certain waiting sovereigns.
Shaking up my soul with a senseless bone sought solving
perfect possible partner.
How could I have fought so hard against recognizing
you, not the physical perfect person, but the principal
perfect version of the perfect possible present."

During the late eighty's during the last few years of her life, someone
she knew was about to go to jail for an extended stay. He allowed her
to use his lovely home with a view and a heated pool on Eagles Nest
road in Hurley, NY for a few years. She was sick but could still load
a wood-stove, and the heated pool was a great therapy.

I would visit often and my kids loved the pool. They would bring
their friends from the city, some of whom had never been out of
Manhattan. Some of these kids from the lower east side were
frowned upon by the local pool owners. Karen made them all feel
welcome anytime.

Eventually that tenancy ended. The house was sold in the Early
ninety's and she moved into a house trailer on the same road. It was
to be her final residence. She had good medical care, and friends in
the neighborhood.

Late in the winter of 1993, a social worker showed up at the trailer,
and announced that she was with the "office of aging" and that they
would be taking her from her home and putting her into a hospice to
die.

Karen called me. "Can they do that ?" she asked. "I want to die at
home" she said. I said I was sure they couldn't against her will and
began negotiators with the Ulster County Department of Social
Services, who now wanted her declared "incompetent" and wanted to

remover her from her home forcibly, saying she was a danger to herself.

They were threatening a "Guardian ad litum" proceeding in local Supreme Court if she continued to refuse to co-operate.

As a legally trained person (Baruch Paralegal Certificate) but not a member of the NY Bar I couldn't make court appearances, but I worked with a lawyer who could. It was OK for a non bar member to appear for someone within the state and county social service system, so I called for a "fair hearing" and appeared on her behalf at a meeting of several female bureaucrats.

The "Office of Aging" was trying to expand their bureaucratic fief, and had taken to visiting old people in the community less for reasons of assistance and more and more the issue seemed to be about who was in control of their lives, the Agency or the individual. The Office of Aging, and the Department of Social Services were attempting to exert control in areas that were clearly constitutionally protected. Their were ugly rumors about senior citizens being removed from their homes and their property looted and sold. Forced dislocations created real estate opportunities, and the sharks were always circling and hungry.

Karen's case was a good case in point. The worker had arrived a unannounced and uninvited, at her door. Karen, being courteous, allowed her in for a "chat". The worker noticed a wire running along the backside of the Sink to an appliance on the kitchen counter.

Based on this observation she was attempting to have Karen declared a "danger to herself" and wanted the Department of Social services to take custody of her and force her into the Hospice to die, "for her own good". The argument was that she had been observed with an electrical wire in her sink and because of this she was therefore incompetent and in "eminent and immediate danger"

The "Fair Hearing" was held in the county office building conference room. Because of the number of departments involved the long table looked like something out of a movie set. Karen was much too sick to attend, and I found my self facing nearly a dozen grim faced bureaucratic woman with their female supervisors and department heads. It seemed like they all had a dog in this fight. This was about turf.

The original social worker was angry and defensive over being challenged especially in front of so many of her peers and superiors. All she really had was an observation of a wire near the sink and a very sick Karen. I pointed out that the alleged danger of the unsafe wire was born out of ignorance. The social worker obviously didn't know how wiring worked and was conjuring up an image of a threat that didn't exist. The wire was grounded and it was a normal practice to plug appliances in near a sink, that's why there was an outlet there, and that even if the wire been running into the water in the sink and not just passed it the wire was still properly grounded and furthermore was plugged into a "ground fault interrupter circuit".

Also Karen was in the personal care of an excellent private Doctor. Social Services had no jurisdiction over Karen, her life, or her illness. I told them that I would like to make a statement, for the record. I still remember the sun coming through the windows as I made eye contact with each of them around the table and said "I can't believe that its 1993, and I am sitting in a room entirely filled with women except for me. And you, a group of women, in this day and age, of liberation and freedom of choice for women, their bodies, and their lives, would deny this person (Karen), a women, the right to die in her own home.

I assure you of one thing however, that if you persist and are successful with what you are planning for this woman, I will be sure that each and everyone of you personally and the agencies that you work for will be defending lawsuits for years to come."

This threat had some credibility for three reasons. My work in hard-ball litigation for the Taxi fleets in Manhattan had enabled me to generate a summons and complaint in twenty minutes or less. A 27 page discovery demand from the City of NY was breakfast fodder at the time. Besides my own supervising distinguished world class attorney and friend Chris Basler, I knew and occasionally played for benefits for cases and causes involving William Kunstler, the famous civil rights trial attorney.

I also had a track record of suing local public officials in Federal Court. In terms of my attitude it probably didn't hurt that at that time I was sharing NYC offices with Ramsey Clark. Ramsey was the former Attorney General under President Carter and the son of a Supreme Court Justice Clark. His office did the biggest civil rights cases, and the most desperate ones. It was a great honor to work next to those guys.

Bill Kunstler had recently destroyed a County Supreme Court Judge in the same county Karen lived in. He had appeared on behalf of a friend in local court and called the judge a "Sexist Pig". He stated that he had women witnesses and the judge was unfit to hear their testimony. He asked that the judge recuse himself for that reason.

When threatened with contempt Kunstler argued that the truth was his defense and he could prove his point. He argued that the judge was in fact a sexist pig and the judges ex-wife and several of her friends were willing to testify to that fact.

The local bureaucrats were terrified of the high powered eminent council from NY. The last thing they wanted was scrutiny, litigation, and worst of all publicity.
Faced had to be saved, but they S.S ladies caved. The Department of Social Services agreed that Karen would stay in her home, but the social worker would come by in a week or so to "check and make sure she is OK". I agreed but insisted that they would have to give notice and that I would be there to prevent any other false allegations.

A little over a week later I got a notice that the social worker wanted to schedule a visit. I set a time and went over to visit Karen the night before. The social worker was coming around 11:AM. I remember that I hugged Karen goodnight by the door and was surprised by how thin she was, and the wave of heat that emanated from her frail form.

The next day I got there about 10:30, I knocked and let my self in. Karen appeared to be sleeping. I figured she probably needed the rest and decided not to wake her for half an hour. I sat and watched the price is right on the TV that was on in the living room next to the bed. Bob barker had just awarded the final showcase prizes and I knew it was coming to the end of the half hour so I decided to wake Karen. I shook her shoulder but she didn't move.

 It was a strange feeling because I didn't know what to do. I picked up the phone next to the bed and called Bob Brainen's house. His girl friend answered. I said "she's not moving" and she said "call the Doctor". The Doctor's number was by the phone so I did and spoke briefly with the Doctor. He said to check for breathing and pulse. When they were negative he said she was gone.

The Doctor then made a call to the County Coroner and the State Police. In a few minutes Trooper Manly of the NY State Troopers arrived followed by 1st the Coroner and then the Social worker who arrived late to find all this activity in progress. Trooper Manly took the report, and the Coroner got out a body bag.   We lifted the body into the bag, When we moved the body it appeared that rigor was just beginning to set in and the lividity on the lower side of the body made it obvious that she had been dead for hours.

The trooper followed procedure by the book and less then an hour later it was all over and done. I went home to write her obituary and send it to the local papers. It was the only thing I could think of to do.

Months later I was looking through a box of files that she had given me. I found a brochure that she had saved. It included a picture of me playing harmonica with the old guard of the "Grand Old O'pry. at one of the early Newport Festivals, and an original "Boston Broadside" with my picture on the cover.   She had been thoughtful enough to save these things for me for almost 45 years. It reminded me of her 1969 Album:

"It's so hard to tell who's gonna love you the best."

QUOTES AND PRAISE

"My favorite singer in the place was Karen Dalton. She was a tall white blues singer and guitar player, funky, lanky, and sultry. I'd actually met her before. I'd run across her the previous summer outside of Denver I a mountain pass town in a folk club. Karen had a voice like Billie Holiday's and plays guitar like Jimmy Reed and went all the way with it. I sang with her a couple times" - Bob Dylan

"She sure can sing the shit out of the blues" - Fred Neil

"Without a doubt she is my favorite singer". - Devendra Banhart

"Sounds less like a folk record and more like a warp in the space-time continuum. A portal that links prehistoric blues with the freakiest acoustic music being made today. It's also the most beautiful and harrowing album you'll hear this year" –
John Lewis, Uncut Magazine

"A devastating personification of despair, a haunting exchange between voice and guitar, her ghostly whine and mournful voice as otherworldly as Delta blues singer Skip James and the Blue grass patriarch Ralph Stanley. A case can be made for Karen Dalton, the late Greenwich Village folkie sometimes referred to as the best singers nobody's heard, as the archetype of the current pop-cabaret stylists Norah Jones and Madeleine Peyroux, Even Leslie Feist". - Bill Friskies-Warren, Washington Post

"Her talent is raw, but her mesmerizing versions of blues, R&B and fold songs are unforgettable. You could literally feel the pain and suffering in every line she sang."
 - Mark Regenstreif Montreal Gazette

"She understood the blues better than the folk singing milieu she was hanging out with. Absolutely she's a blues singer to me. It's full of

idiosyncrasies that you can't repeat – it's in her voice and its just extraordinary. She's my absolute favorite blues singer. -
 Nick Cave, Capital records

"Karen Dalton sang the blues better than anyone before or since" - Dusted Magazine

"Like blues maverick John Lee Hooker,, Dalton's pained cry follows such a deeply
Individualized sense of rhythm and melody that the songs heave and lunge like ocean waves breaking on a rock strewn beach" - The Scene

You can feel the atmosphere in the room – they're hanging on every syllable Dalton utters, her breath is keeping the whole space together, transfixed on the songs as they emerge, fully formed and free..the songs breathe so terribly honestly. She accompanies her dark straight and fucking beautiful true voice, picking out the kind of melodies that make you ache to want to be there. Her legendary arrangements amaze time after time. Her songs sound imbedded in the singers life, her own experience – but whether of not the person of Dalton, her actual self is in these songs is beside the point, because she brings their characters, tragedies, scope and joy straight into the instant unfolding existence. She see's it happening, it's happening to her – whatever, it's there, right in front of your eyes, she brings it to you" - Foxy Digitalis

"An intimate, candlelit mood that's simultaneously unbearably sad and life affirming" - Q

 "Unique – literally" - the Guardian

"Words like classic and genius are tossed around far too readily, in this instance, they don't tell half the story – Evening Standard

"Bone chilling wonderful" - The New York Times

"One of the most influential musicians of her time"   - Bust Magazine

"Genre-defying and utterly unique, a dusky jewel" Harp Magazine"

"4 stars – hypnotic" - Playboy

"A voice that could make the statues cry" SF Weekly

"Like Dylan before her, she make sense of the whole sprawling territory of "American popular music: rock folk, jazz, country, blues, cabaret, and whatever else she could wrap her voice around." - Chicago Reader

"A major archeological find, with Dalton at last the equal of her gilded contemporaries Five stars out of five" - The Times

POEMS AND SONGS

The writings in this collection fall into three basic category's:

1) Songs she collected
2) What she wrote (songs and poems)
3) What she performed

I have divided them into several parts;

The first is is songs and poems by Karen

The second two parts are blues and folk lyrics most of which are in the public domain except where authorship is known and noted. Some traditional songs have been modified, transcribed, or arranged by Karen in which case the rights to the arrangements and stylizations remain the property of the artist.

The third part is songs by other people. Some of these are in the original handwriting of the author, others are transcribed from handwritten copies of the chord changes and lyrics. Others with clear copyright and publishing info are listed with author, and/or publisher.

The last part is Karen's "song lists" and "Gig sheets" for her performances.

Every method has been made to give appropriate Songwriting and Publishing credit, and persons wishing to use any of this material that is copyright protected are urged to get in touch with the original author or publisher where possible. Harry Fox licensing and BMI/ASCAP "song search" is a good way to go about this for licensing, covers, sampling, etc. Any material presented herein is for archival and reference purposes only. For licenses in regard to Karen's songs, poetry etc. they are listed with Harry Fox Agency NYC, NY

Karen was scrupulously careful to notate the author of the songs in her repertoire. Where she omitted credits it was because the source was unidentified or the song was her original work.

She often referred to herself as "a song stylist". Drawing from folk roots, her own writings, and modern pop classics she made every song uniquely her own.
She wrote many entirely new songs but except for one, they were unrecorded.
If somehow I have given her credit for the work of another, or have failed to appropriately credit the source, forgive me please. Polite requests for changes and credits will be honored.

The good news is that the miracle of modern publishing allows for swift updates and corrections

In going through the tattered fragments of fading paper contained in the pile of file folders representing Karen's life's work arranging and collecting music relevant to her generation, one becomes aware of being in the presence of a genuine root folk source.

Transcribing these fragile, mostly handwritten, musty, crumbling notes of Karen's has been a distinctly enlightening experience. Each song was selected for a reason, and those reasons become obvious as one delves deeper into her collection and writings. Each of Karen's songs creates a moment, stops time, brings to life forgotten chapters in our own history.

I sometimes wonder if this old friend of mine, was aware of how important she was. It was her honesty and her taste that made her infallible in one very important area. She knew what the poignant quality was that made some music great and others just something else. She collected the great ones. The blues lyrics that tear your heart out. The lyrics that make moments happen in the heart. She wrote songs. She wrote poetry, She wrote. When too sick to sing, she wrote.

It becomes clear, sorting through these fading scraps of my friends life that she was dedicated to love and beauty and the magic that a song could make happen.

She was at her best when she was perceiving what was great and pure about a song and then using the magic of the muted breaking trumpet of her voice she announced each line clearly, but you could hear her heart breaking inside her as she identified with the feelings of the author of the song. In that way she was magical, It was her greatness. That she could do that, and suffer in real time with both the writer and the listener communicating a heart breaking story with a bent tone sliding up to pitch, a break in the time, a raw honesty. She took songs and transformed them into something of her own. In doing so she broke through a time and space barrier to greatness.

At the end she said "its not my fault". No it wasn't. Maybe it was just bad luck. Perhaps chemicals were the only relief she had from the pain of her existence, other peoples pain, the blind, the lost authors of the blues lyrics, lost lovers and friends, you and me. She could feel our pain in her own private world of torment and love.

So, here they are; the songs, poems, and fragments that embodied the life and spirit of the wonderful person that was Karen Dalton

SONGS AND POEMS BY KAREN

"Early one morning, the blues slipped away, and left me no place to hide in Colorado" K.D.

POEM FOR A STRUNG OUT POET   By: Karen
Dalton

Not Dead yet, not dead, and love not dead
Fix a tragic mask on bitter spikes
Gods unholy face may fall

Gibber down bloody fallen tunnels
Echoing all madness, not dead yet,
Crossing old rivers of no concern

Riding dreams behind comatose Indian eyes
To holy countries of no rain
Love you are so beautiful
Sleeping through the first April storm

Remembering pain,
Unwatching eyes, remembering
Impaled upon that utmost evil
Not dead yet

Guarding overgrown gardens of forgotten paradise
Walking in the cold green wind
It will be spring now, soon
Soon it will be spring.

April, 1961 NYC

STAR SONG   by: Karen Dalton

Just letting the moon go
Where the day has gone
I'm dreaming away
Being high and full of love

And while the sky is full of little stars
I'm dreaming about you
And your eyes
Dreaming a star song

My song making it do to pass
The time along
Waiting for you
And nothing can go wrong

When I'm making up my song
Singing a sky song
Just letting the day do
What it must come to

I'm floating away
Being high and full of love
The sky is blue with little clouds
I'm thinking about you
And your eyes
And singing this sky song

(key of G) changes: G – D7 – G – C – A – D – G

DON'T MAKE IT EASY   By: Karen Dalton

Little regrets are so hard to forget
I may take my time forgetting you
Cause loving you the way I do
Don't make it easy

Things that you said, don't leave my head

I may take my time forgetting you
And loving you the way I do
Don't make it easy

You could be wrong and wait too long
Trying to see what you've been to me
It's so hard when I just keep missing you
Don't make it easy

MET AN OLD FRIEND   By: Karen Dalton

Met an old friend the other day
He was so sorry that I'd gone astray
He asked me if I needed help
I told him to go help himself

My sin was the sweetest love
That's what I'll be thinking of
My sin was the sweetest love
That's what I'll be thinking of

Went to see the folks at home
They said I'd been doing wrong
When they said they would forgive
That's when I said live and let live

My sin was the sweetest love
That's what I'll be thinking of
My sin was the sweetest love
That's what I'll be thinking of

When I'm old and ready to die
I won't scream and I wont cry
I'll take with me what I know
Tell the angels that I loved him so

My sin was the sweetest love
That's what I'll be thinking of
My sin was the sweetest love

That's what I'll be thinking of

WAITING FOR YOU   By: Karen Dalton

I was waiting for you today
Thinking of how we used to be
What did we say
Waiting become much longer
Although I used to wait forever

Now with all the hours that we spent together gone
I just don't want to go on never saying it
I just can't stay at home alone
And I just don't want to go on
Waiting for you

TOPANGA CANYON   By: Karen Dalton

Lover of tears crying, rain trickling secret rocks
Trees reaching away walls, rotting cliffs,
Leaves, fear, ashes, earth
Lover of music screaming discord
In old forgotten caves

I beyond recognition, I
Weep the sharpened edge of my confessions
Lover of fear, shuddering out flung arms
Bleeding from flowers of self-denial where
We lay naked in the night
And did not love

Far down the sea was turning sand
The fog hanging ragged points
The perilous narrow road
The cast up starfish

LONG WAY HOME   By: Karen Dalton

"Lets take the long way home" you said
So we rode along the rocky way

The water used to go

Under to evergreen trees
Down someplace where I can't follow
You cast your mind around, imagining ideas
Dreaming of clear water

"Take of your rings" you said
And stay with me
The flowers will be remembered from this day
And we'll have a secret then
Before they fade away

About those tears that might have been
For the love I'm in.

GRAVITY AND TIME   By: Karen Dalton

They struggled up the mountain in the yellow September heat
Thru the dry grass and more cactus until at last
The little sliding rocks and the spaces of boulders

Trickles of sweat ran through the child's hair
Tears, anger, impotence, fear mingled dust on her face
Her girls body struggled against gravity and time

GOT MY NEW DRESS   By Karen Dalton
I've got my new dress, put it on
I don't care where the old one's gone
I've got it, put it on

Gone to wear it on home
I need to use it just to hang around downtown
Or if I'm passing by with my friend
I've got it, put it on

MOSES   By: Karen Dalton

Old arms twisted toward paling sun
And come white water walls

Against the sweat-tear stained dusty feet

Prints washed away, filled
The marks of old arches still strong
Salt again stinging old brown skin

The starfish curls a little at the edges, dies
On some far washed beach, starlight
Should not come to close

SOMETIMES I WISH I WAS IN LOVE   By: Karen Dalton

Sometimes I wish I was in love again
But I can't be with you while you treat me this way
Every time I wish to be where I was then
I think and then I know you'll never stay

Love life to you means less then living
At least the way I see it you don't care
I know that my mind is past receiving
Anything you think that I should share

All the tears and open hurt we've shown so far
Doesn't make the pain an easy load

WORDS THAT GO TOGETHER WELL   By: Karen Dalton

Words that go together well are

Like those fine phrases

Used with sullen gazes

At someone you used to know.

And at final parting noting

Which words you choose to say

The things you choose to say.

Those words that go together well

Are areas worth taming

And the taming sometimes changes

But always rearranges

The things you choose to lose

ONE SONG GONE   By: Karen Dalton

Taken morning evening afternoon of unbelievable sequence. What thoughts actions etc? Taken me looking at looking at looking at mirror me, fake me impossible, incredible grotesque simile me real me ugly me there you have it!!! Ugly me that I feel sorry for and take such great care of. My knowing why my sister hates me not enough now I have to find out why I die so hard. If I die the music will stop, time stopping perhaps to realize that last thing, the thing (whatever it is) that I was doing last perpetuated round forever like some idiots song.
Confess my reality. (here I sit, full of shit) confess that I am demon inhabited and write in parenthesis.

Time as may is, time as may be
Space being that forgotten past
Space being the train missed
After it was gone, what thinking now, what thinking
forty miles of screams and the pauses in between days wait
Days done done done where done
Finished now gone gone to be remembered to remember
I remember some sound face feeling,
Then time burns bright again and marks on me on my face.
Hang time hanging time dangling time suspended
Ah, that's it, stopped and hang on some no quite heard sound

Remembering over and over that it is not possible to remember
Forgotten one song more

SO LONG AGO AND FAR AWAY   By: Karen Dalton

Passing time within every minute
Hours count each day
Rain and sunshine all may be
So long ago and far away

Loves illusion dreams may change
Games that we all play

Friends and lovers all become
So long ago and far away

Could you promise me
Would you promise me
Could it ever be, that you could stay?

REMEMBERING MOUNTAINS   By: Karen Dalton

C – D – C – D – C – D – C

Sun will fall across the canyon wall
C - D – C - D
My prayer on every stone and tree
G – D – G – D – Bf – D – C
Let the last be beauty, all in beauty, all in beauty
D   C
Now your time is your own
        D
You'll be alone
                G
And sit in your room
        C   D
Remembering mountains
G   C   D
Do you think the seasons changed

Without your heart
   G   D
Are you dreaming
    Bf   C   D
Every day and night will come to your mind
    C - D
Undeceiving
   D
You will know
             C   D
There is no parting without sorrow

So you sit by the window
Watching the days go by
Alone in your room
Remembering Mountains

Do you think of all the ways
you didn't follow, are you dreaming

Every way will lead you on
To find tomorrow
I'm believing

You'll find tomorrow brings
You to return

HAPPY JOSE   Traditional: Argmt; K.D.

In Mexico there lives an old fellow
Everyone knows him as Happy Jose
And if you ask what he grows in his garden
He'll just smile and then he will say

(Cho)
Oh, what we grow in old Mexico

Oh, what we grow in old Mexico

Happy Jose doesn't have any worries
He grows enough for his own simple needs
And if he finds that he makes a few pesos
He goes to his garden and harvest some weeds
(Cho)

One day there came two Federalistas
To investigate Jose's dubious fame
He gave them two cigarillos
And pretty soon they forgot why they came
(Cho)

Now Jose lives in a big Hacienda
All his servants are happy and gay
They work for hours and never stop smiling
And all he pays is a nickel a day   (Cho)

GALLERY   By: Karen Dalton

    I.   Statuary has no meaning
        Other than like the emotional impact of words
        Driving mi into considerations that I never intended
        By formal presentations of fussy concepts

    II. Even these, demanding I think what some creator
        Inspired and probably pathetic and sordid
        Viewed as truth and made a monument in marble or bronze
        Abstractly communicates

    III. I have seen mountains and know more
        Walking hugely on my own uncertain lumpy feet
        Between rocks of no certain Formfullness
        Where I alone set limitations
        On Purposefullness

THE LOST ARE FOUND   By; Karen Dalton

(Cmaj – Emi – Ef – Af6 – Gsus4 – G7

Cma7   Fmi7
Standing by the well wishing for the rain rain rain,
A
Reaching to the clouds
F   Bf   G79
For nothing else remains
C
Drifting in a daze
Emi7
When evening will be done
Ami
Try looking through a haze
Ami/G F   Bf G79 Bf7
At an empty house in the cold cold sun
E6   Ef7
I will wait until it all goes around
Af7
With you in sight
Cmi/G
The lost are found
(play) Cmaj7 – C add 9

NATURAL WOMAN   Karen Dalton

He thought I was a savior
He thought I'd come to tidy up
The loose ends that were his mind

I never thought to ask him how he chose me
I only asked him how much he
Was willing to leave behind

He thought I was a halo
He thought I'd bring his mantra down
He thought that my shit don't stink

And I had to blow his mind completely
And swamp him with my feet of clay
So he would have room to think

(Bridge:)
And see that I'm just a natural woman
As he simply a natural man
But somehow, within this sad human frame
I'm going to give him the best I can

And every day he's learning
He's not so quick to sit and judge
Without knowing all the facts

Every day in little ways he's growing
I see it in his smile and in
The kindness with which he acts

And maybe I'm a savior
And maybe I'm a chump, you know
It's getting so hard to tell

And maybe he and I have saved each other
And maybe when he looks at me next time
He will see me well

(Repeat Bridge:)
And see that I'm just a natural woman
As he simply a natural man
But somehow, within this sad human framework
I'm going to give him the best I can

INSIDE YOUR LOVING EYES   By: Karen Dalton

C#mi   Bmi
I tried to tell you
 C#   Bmi   C

It all comes true inside your loving eyes
   D   A   G
Some little thing you might have said
  C#mi   Bmi   C#
For dear loves sake

Everything that you have done
Means love to me now more then it did then
Some little thing you might have done
For a dear loved one

Release:
    D   C#   Bmi   C#
Times of memories stay with me
    D   C#   C   C#
As the days are passing

   Bmi   C#
I'll find everything I want to be
    D   E   A   G
In the promises you eyes made to me

Believing as I would have been
To make that music live again for you
Trying to tell you it all comes true
Inside your loving eyes

C#mi – Bmi – D – E – A – G

Bmi – Ami – C – D – G – F -

Release: C – Bmi – Ami – Bmi – C – Bmi – Bf – Bmi – Ami – Bmi –
C – D- G – F

LEFT HANDED LADIE   Karen Dalton

Left handed ladie, eyes so bright
What do you dream of tonight
Do you wait for the strong man to

Carry you to safety do you feel
The pulse of the rocking chair.
Are you aware of your deepest and
Truest emotions like an ocean of despair.
No, I don/t despair though
I'm often lonely if only
Someone spoke the language out there
Perhaps I/ll walk along the river
Moon-shadows on moss beds
Find a companion where A fallen log lies over a doorway
To the realms of never never land.. ..
Seed, I'll never-nevet-land in your world
Of numbers time ticking by while
reality slumbers like a behemoth
Unspirited and ungainly - mainly I'm
Happy with the whole of the lair
Left-handed ladie in the night
Why for you do the flames glow bright
Like the candlelight your soul is flickering
Tween the worlds of here and the after life
Condemned for an attitude
It's hard to believe you were in the
Nude – rags burnt and hair flying
So beautiful as you were dying
Left handed ladie take me to never – never land

ALL THAT SHINES IS NOT TRUTH   Karen
Dalton

All that shines is not truth
All that glitters does not shine
Real Beauty rarely glitters -so I find

Broken diamonds on the floor
Fractured beauties enter violence
Muddy waters search for shore
Despite the mist

Lovely ladies clothed in crimson
Talking of the days to come

Never noticing that they're missing the finding of
A Prince in the glowing silver
A cross upon his chest
Tossed aside with a crown of paper, truly blessed

A Shepard waits in woolen garments
Fallen leaves Float in the rain
The mud must soak my garments
I'm too clean

FOR THE LOVE I'M IN   Karen Dalton
(late 60's)

When we were there the flowers grew everywhere
All along the mountains
Lets take the long road home you said
So we rode around the rocky way
The water used to go

Under the evergreen trees
Down someplace where I can't follow
You cast your mind around imagining ideas
Dreaming of clear water.

Take of your rings you said
And stay with me
The flowers will be remembered
And we'll have a secret then
From the day before they fade away
About those flowers that might have been
For the love I'm in

MORNINGS   Karen Dalton

Perhaps when I awoke screaming
I was only from a dream misunderstood
Reality , not down-curving to
Evil inescapably through some
Unnoticed conversation remembered
In the night

I have sometimes been between walls
Of unfamiliar windows or seen the
Cages of strange cities with tired
Night – opened eyes, or sometimes in
Linoleum hotels when time lies at
The bottom of a sticky wine bottle,
I, sick for home, I remember the
Other mornings.

Hope there will not come a time
When I lie wakeful and my feet drawn
In supplication against the cold
Of a morning
In some darkened stained – shaded room
That I may not come to lie alone
On some huge bed
Naked by myself at some
Morning past midday, gettin old

I have walked on many rain-running sidewalks
Fumbling my fragile dreams among
Neglected neon rainbows
And lost them there.
Sometime I dream that I will fall
Into morning shouting sensuality
Somewhere other than mornings of
Obscene afternoon lights
Not see my face pale in
A dusty mirror
Waiting for evening

It cannot be that mornings of
Promise have passed
It is not true that reality sung and crashed
Unheard music in silence through
Some room where I no longer live
Or blew wind-songs through high
Unfamiliar doorways
Where I will never stand.

ONLY AHEAD (CAN LAY THE DREAM)   Karen Dalton

We must rise towards ourselves
Reach inward for strength
Seek courage in our faith
Run towards joy
Gazing backwards at darkness

For only ahead can lay the dream
And our hearts and minds alone
Can carry us there.

A WAKING VISION   Karen Dalton

I recognized a waking vision... the vision
I've conjured since memory began
The spirit living in fairy tale hero's.
The familiar shoulder just out of reach of my clasp.

The river boy, dream companion,
The soldier who romanced the lady
The shadows of my nite lite,
The father, lover, in my miniature world.
You're waiting as I recover, numb,
Hopeless, spent, sick with an amnesia of
The soul.

You are inevitable – to deny you, the
Image that haunted my life would be
Like trying to alter a memory.

AT LAST THE NIGHT HAS ENDED   Karen Dalton

At last the night has ended,
I grew old while the rain fell down
I thank you for this memory
And the peaceful quiet sound

Rain hits the window

My lovers eyes are closed
A symphony of gladness
I'm trying to compose

I've heard falseness screaming louder
Then it's ever been before
Whatever it takes to forget it
I will keep it from my door

Falseness leads to apathy
Apathy leads to fate
Fate sneaks up from behind
Pretty soon it's too late
To stand in anyone else's shoes
Without being able to run.

BEFORE THE JUDGE   Karen Dalton

My word is my honor
It needs no defense
No empty oath
Makes recompense
To my mind and my heart
Carved from the rock
Upon my own path
I always shall walk

Yes it's true
Yes it's true

There's no battle I can't win
As long as I'm proud
As long as I'm proud
I'll always have a place to live

This is my prayer
A speech in a can
I built this cloud
That I stand upon
Made of illusion

And a life long dose
To explore my fate
And find my place

Yes it's real
Yes it's real
I feel it so it must be true
My spirit is free
My spirit is free
There's no thing I can't

My innocence stands'
And guards my pride
No need to bow down
No need to hide

The future will come
The future will fade
I will not seek shelter
I will not be afraid

Whatever you say, what ever you say
I will not doubt the truth I have known
My soul and myself, myself and my soul
No one shall ever own.

MISTAKES THUS FAR: Karen Dalton

Too much confidence
Refusal to sacrifice security
Fear of failure
Stagnation
No effort to expand yourself
Let yourself get distracted
Haven't given it your all
Listened to too many people
All of then are wrong
Except those words you can remember
Stayed in one place

Thinking anyone cares about you
Thinking that your youth will last forever
Thinking you will succeed in that effort

THE REMEDY   Karen Dalton

Be humble but strong
Walk on the tightrope
Seek danger/challenge
You cannot fail – Know It   - Move
Use the phone, write letters
Make a tape and send it everywhere
FOCUS it is your gift
No one else can take it
Give it all you have
Until you can't and then
Give more
Seek no advice
Listen to nothing but your heart
Branch out, let them know you exist
Someone does!
The effort bears the fruit

4 hours a day! 6 hours a day! Do it or die!

I'LL FOLLOW YOU   Karen Dalton

I'll follow you
I'll follow you
Just tell me where you'll go
We cannot be wandering
Down this road

Through the cold wind and snow
We met we met on a sunny day
When the summer was high and blooming
he leaves have fallen up0n there way

A winter too fierce now is looming

We walked we walked both hands entwined
past eyes that had looked way past us
Something that precious can't be defined
For not forever can it last us.

I'll prove my love, I'll prove my love to you
When time has past and we've fallen
Tis then I will sing that these words are all true
You will hear me proudly call

Behold, behold, my second hand rags
Thread bare and the winter is coming
But the rags they are warm beside your heart
And under the tune you are humming

Please, oh please, stay beautiful
For It's your beauty that I have seen
I shall never forget the gift of you
Though long lost the battle been

MY STRINGS AWAKE   Karen Dalton

My strings awake! Perform the task
labor that you and I shall grasp
And end what I have now begun
For when this song is sung and past
And strings be still, for I have done

As to be heard an none has known
As fragments of a greater stone
My song may pierce her heart of stone
Should we hen sigh, sing or moan?
No, no my strings for I have done.

The rocks do not so cruelly
Repulse the waves continually
As my win of perfection
So hat I am past the remedy
And so my strings and I have done

Vengeance shall fall on thy disdain
That makes but a game of honest pain
Think not alone under the sun
But seek a shelter from the rain
As my strings and I have done

THIS IS OUR LOVE   Karen Dalton

A typewriter smashed upon a rock
A Shepard leading his faithful flock
This is our love, this is our love

A morning spent waiting for the sun
A nasty thief left for to run
This is our love, this is our love

A flower blooming in barren ground
A silent word that makes no sound
This is our love, this is our love

An island in an angry storm
A summer breeze sweet and warm
This is our love, this is our love

Bad news in a time of need
New root from a peaceful seed
This is our love, this is our love

A full moon in an open sky
A wounded dove that cannot fly
This is our love, this is our love

A choir of angels with no song
A winding road steep and long
This is our love, this is our love

A saint of honor with lands concealed
A bird loose in a barley field
This is our love, this is our love

A summer spent barefoot and free
A foolish soul who fails to see
This is our love, this is our love

A saint of honor with lands concealed
Knows nothing but his prayers and dreams
His vision soon will be revealed
His tattered rags redeemed
Walking always never rides
His speech it soundly crashes
A poor lost soul to him confides
That in a lonely sea he thrashes

MY LOVE MY LOVE   Karen Dalton

My love, my love
I will watch you
I watch you, watch you grow
From a child of shimmer
To a goddess of the snow
To a goddess of the snow

My love, my love
I'll listen to you cry
I'll hear you weep so softly
Far away from the place where I lie
Far away from the place where I lie

My love, my love
I'll make a promise
That strong shall never fade
We will build upon a foundation
That our hearts and heads have made
That our hearts and heads have made

My love, my love
I will follow
I will follow your winding trail
I'll carry your weight for ever
Together we shall not fail
Together we shall not fail

My love, my love
I will hold you
I hold you while the cold winds blow
The darkness will pound upon the rooftop
But the light will come I know
But the light will come I know

My love, my love
I will see you
I will see you break free from your past
It's hell not be left to linger
For nothing of guilt can last
For nothing of guilt can last

My love, my love
I will find you
I will find you in a great garden
I will come to you upon my knees
Like a beggar seeking pardon
Like a beggar seeking pardon

My love, my love
I will remember
I will remember your beautiful love
Swirling through the meadow
I will not pass up my chance
I will not pass up my chance

My love, my love
I will play you
Softly like an ancient lute
I will whisper so only you can hear
That my love has laid it's root

That my love has laid it's root

My love, my love
I will inhale you
As the wind of the summer past
Through my soul your spirit flowing
While this youth slips away so fast
While this youth slips away so fast

My love, my love
I will hear you
I will hear you softly sing
Upon a morning cold and bright
I will hand you a golden ring
I will hand you a golden ring

My love, my love
I will touch you
I will touch you where none can see
The night will explode all around us
And through it we shall be free
And through it we shall be free

My love, my love
I will catch you if you should stumble
We will walk away with no regret
So proud so young so humble
So proud so young so humble

My love, my love
I will protect you
I will protect you from all you fear
You shall forget your troubles
When close I draw you near
When close I draw you near

BEFORE THE SPIRIT FINDS IT'S PLACE   Karen Dalton
What in vain has to be won
What glory can exceed the sun
For how long must a spirit run

Until it finds it's place
Until it finds it's place

How much darkness must be seen
How loud must loneliness scream
How long must a spirit dream
Until it finds its place
The answer I am seeking
Is one that I shall find
As the day softly unfolds
And the tangled web unwinds

I'll sit in a smoky corner
Waiting words to tell a tale
Soon the story will be told
I swear I will not fail

What a burden must be lifted
What mountains must be shifted
How much sand must be sifted
Before the spirit finds it's place

How much wealth must be squandered
How many notions must be pondered
How many trails must be wandered
Before the spirit finds it's place

Far has the journey man come
From a cradle that once did fall
Long has he been searching
For a way around the wall
He knows he soon will find it
For he cannot be denied
Something from a truthful heart
Forever cannot hide

What end to the forest unexplored
What final blow must be scored
How much fruit must it remand
Before the spirit finds it's place

What courage must be shown
What heartache must be known
What boulder must be thrown
Before the spirit finds it;s place
Before the spirit finds it's place

THE KINGDOM   Karen Dalton
(11/14/1992)

Who could even hope to rule
The lands the seas the skies
One who claims to hold the throne
Must surely be filled with lies

One cannot hope to chain the land
For upon it all walls will crumble
The land will not except a path
That is guilty of not being humble

One could not dream to still the sea
For the might waves pound their story
With force untold in any great tale
Stand in the way and you'll be sorry.

One could never enslave the skies
For the wind must always be free
The sun and moon planets and stars
Will proclaim how it is to be

This desire will always bring failure
Such tasks will be laid to waste
The trail must be laid so gently
Or else it will surely be erased

The future draws always near
But what one see's one cannot touch
In all the pondering of my youth
At the least I know this much

The throne of the kingdom is empty
Though many will stand in line
Yet no crown shall forever last
Beyond the great grasp of time

SAINT JOHN   Karen Dalton

The word is spoken upon the street
By a man of humble birth
Roaming Sleepless and Shining
He wanders on the earth

Light will accept no darkness
For Darkness cannot prevail
One who seeks to refuse this light
In the end shall only fail
These are the words of a friend of mine

Welcome home my brother
Were the first works I did hear
When I wandered in from the evening trail
With little baggage and so much to fear

Welcome home my brother
Were the first works I did hear
When I wandered in from the evening trail
With little baggage and so much to fear

Two weeks passed by or perhaps more
When upon the grass I slept
A voice said greetings my brother
Too long have the spirits wept

The darkness it seems to be gaining
Yet the light will ever shine
No possession will ever be owned
As nothing will ever be mine

I hold myself above no man and so

I shall always be free
I shall ne'er know the sin of judgment
Nor temptation or jealousy
The cold shall pound at my doorstep
My love will be banished from home
Upon this earth my humble soul
Will have nothing except for to roam
My head may be hung in sorrow
My heart may be pierced by flame
But ne'er shall I suffer defeat
My trails shall not be in vain

These are the words of a friend of mine
These are the words of a friend of mine
A friend of mine

I wish you well dear friend I have not met
I know you'll see things you will not forget
If someday these roads lead to you

ANY FOOL CAN SEE IT   Karen Dalton

Any fool can see it, why can't you
Keep it up, keep on trying, follow your heart
Never stop, never quit, I love you n stuff
You'll make it beautiful on and on and on...
I am becoming a cynic, spoiling this wasteland

A HUMAN MIND   Karen Dalton

For all the things that I will see lay ahead
Because the suffering will bring strength and courage
For the love I will know and learn from
Because the path will lead only to greatness
For the struggle will become relentless, unceasing
The stillness will become torture for a heart
That longs for the heights.
Because the silence can be terrifying and
Time will consume itself
To become power expressed in beauty and divine joy.

This rage will boil and seek revenge against all that has
chained the soul and kept freedom from the heart
It will create motion from nothingness
Life from decay, truth from deception,
The reality from potential and the essence from chaos

All around the fertile mind swirling and rolling
The seas gyrate and press land upon these safe shores.
Attempting to erode all that has been built and all that has grown
only for to stand proud and righteous. .Humanity noble and confused,
 the single soul walks and breathes within. Seeing all that has passed
and gazing into what will come with hope and despair.

Hast the vessel been prepared, has the hull been stocked carefully
With provisions to last through the dark frigid winter?
 I speak not of threatening doom but a cry from somewhere deep
within.
Hast this spirit the endurance to run the course and break
finally free from the hands of fear and failure? What must be left
behind?
What must be gathered? What must be learned?

For my heart be not as a wise confident braggart who claims the
throne
before what lives is preserved, but a soul who from birth has grown
Against all that stood to sway. It is this mystery, the great unknowns,
The waiting legends that weighs so heavy.

Are these the questions of a man lost to youth, or a youth lost to
manhood?
Or is this a moment of metamorphosis, a time of change, a greater
season of growth.
The changes came to fast to grasp and master but too slow to satisfy
the hunger.
This moment is not lost in creation, it is so far from the summit.
Perhaps to climb a mountain one must first stand at it's foot.

I long to prove.
 I long to show.

I long to give
But all within these great hopes lies a trembling body, a sleep that
reveals buried dreams and a mind that is only human

I SEE BEAUTY   Karen Dalton

I see beauty that is not touched
I see love that is not felt
I see truth that is not spoken
Some day it all shall return

I see wisdom that is ignored
I see legends that are not lived
I see grace that is not wanted
Someday this world will learn

FIND OUR WAY   Karen Dalton

I wish you wouldn't say things like that
For they weigh heavy on my mind
In the great search for something to say
That can't be all you can find
I never said that you were to blame
I just said what I thought was true
The sun hasn't even arrived yet
Yet I think this day will be blue
Yes I think this day will be blue

I wish you wouldn't say things like that
Words that you cannot mean
I don't feel like walking out in the cold
]I'd rather be with you in a dream
But words like that they wake me
When I haven't got my rest
We don't need any more weight now
If we want to succeed at this quest
Yeah if we want to succeed at this quest

 I wish you wouldn't say things like that
That there's nothing you can do

I've learned that whatever you believe
Sure enough becomes true

If we really look hard enough
We'll see that we haven't even tried
We haven't prepared for the storm ahead
Its going to be a hell of a ride
It's going to be a hell of a ride

I wish you wouldn't say things like that
Words that strike me like spears
My flesh is not so strong
That it can withstand too many scars

I don't wanna be afraid to lose you
I don't wanna have to run away
But we can't be hurting each other
If we want to find a way
Yeah, if we want to find away

BLUE NOTION   Karen Dalton

There is a blue sky
There is a blue ocean
Staring blue eyes
Staring blue notion

Reach down from heaven
Outside the walls
Outside of heaven, everything falls,
Everything falling, far as I can see

Reach down forever,
Darling take a hold of me
(instrumental break)   F - Ami - D - G - F - Ami - D - G

BLUES SONGS AND LYRICS

I LOVE YOU BABY   Sonny Terry

I love you baby, Baby please don't go
Well I love you baby, baby please don't go. (X2)
Well believe me baby, you know it's gonna hurt me so.

Whoo - hoo =   (X3)

Well I love you baby, gonna tell it all over town (X2)

Want em to know you ain't no hand-me-down
Well he knock me out, wanna tell it everywhere
The way he wear his hair

MISSISSIPPI RIVER BLUES   Hank Snow

Oh you Mississippi river with water so deep and wide
My thoughts of you keep rising just like an evening tide
I'm just like a seagull that has left the sea
Oh your muddy waters keep on calling me.

Chorus: I'm gonna pack my grip and head that way
          You'll see me there again some day
           cause that's the only way to lose
           those Mississippi river blues
           Got the river blues

 I've often ridden on your bosom
From Memphis down to New Orleans
flowing over muddy waters
Drifting through familiar scenes
And when I hear the whistle blow of an old steamboat
Down the river again I'm going to float   -   Chorus:

FEAST HERE TONIGHT   By: Blind man; Argmt, K.D.

There's a rabbit in a log and I ain't got no dawg
How will I get him, I know, I'll get me a briar
And I'll twist it in his hair,
And that's how I'll get him I know

       (chorus) I know, I know
             (repeat last lines of verse)
             (last two lines of verse)

I'll build me a fire and I'll cook that old hare
Roll him up in the flames to make hm brown

I'll fish here tonight while the moon is shining bright
(or) there's a feast here tonight
And find me a place to lay down

       (chorus) I know, I know
             (repeat last lines of verse)
             (last two lines of verse)

I'm going down the track with my coat (or a chicken) on my back
So worn my shoes are nearly gone
Just a little ahead there's a farmers shed
That's where I'll rest my weary bones

       (chorus) I know, I know
             (repeat last lines of verse)
             (last two lines of verse)

BLACK SNAKE MOAN   By: Blind Lemon

Ooh, better run that black snake down
Ooh, better run that black snake down
O seem my mama, black snake send her away from town

Ooh, black snake so hard to find
Ooh, black snake so hard to find

I don't worry about my mama
Can't keep her off my mind

Ooh, better find my mama soon
Ooh, better find my mama soon
Black snake was a-making a ruckus in my room

Ooh black snake is evil, black snake is all I see
Ooh black snake is evil, black snake is all I see
I woke up this mornin, black snake has moved in on me.

Ooh, black snake was hanging around
Ooh, black snake was hanging around
The other side my livin room and broke my pocket book down

WALKING BLUES   Traditional

Paper boy's hollering extra, have you heard the news
Lord I just shot the man I love, got them walking blues
I keep on walking, trying to walk the blues away
Well, I.m so glad, trouble won't last always.

Got grounds in my coffee, Boll weevils in my meal
Tacks in my left shoe, keep sticking in my heel
I keep on walking, trying to walk my blues away

Nobody cares about me, ain't even got a friend
Lord I lost my mother, when will my troubles end

Blues in the Morning, Blues in the afternoon
Blues when it's midnight, why do you come so soon.

MAKE ME A PALLET ON YOUR FLOOR   Traditional

Make me a pallet on your floor,
Make me a pallet on your floor,
Must make me a pallet, make it down on your floor
If your girl comes, I swear she will never know

Just make it, baby,, make it very soft and low
Just make it, baby,, make it very soft and low
If you feel like lying down with me, on the pallet on the floor
And if your girl comes, I swear she will never know

I'll get up in the morning and make you a red hot meal
I'll get up in the morning and make you a red hot meal
Just to show you I appreciate it what you have done for me
When you made me a pallet on your floor

Make it baby, make it very soft and low,
Make it baby make it by the kitchen door
If your girl comes in the front door
I swear she will never know
That you made me a pallet on your floor

THESE ARE MY BLUES   Traditional

My baby woke up this morning with his face all full of frowns
My baby woke up this morning with his face all full of frown
He said honey I'm gonna leave you
This evening when the sun goes down

I tried to talk to my baby, when his friend is not around
I tried to talk to my baby, when his friend is not around
He said "I'm still gonna leave you
This evening when the sun goes down"

Now my bed is so hard, have to lay on by myself
Now my bed is so hard, have to lay on by myself
And that man I been loving all this time with
Laying somewhere else

These are my blues, sing em anywhere I please
These are my blues, sing em anywhere I please

Sing 'em on land or waterThey give my poor heart ease..

BLUE RAILROAD TRAIN   Traditional

   I. Blue railroad train going down the railroad tracks
     Makes me feel so doggone blue to listen to that old smoke stack
     Drivers rolling on leaving me here behind
     Get me back to the good old days
     And let me ramble down the line

  II. Blue railroad train leaving me here alone
     Treat me bad, treat me good making me think of home
     Oh that lonesome train, I love to hear the whistle blow
     Taking the sun leaving the rain and making me want to go

 III. I got the blues longing for company
     Its many miles to where I am but your the one for me
     Its so lonesome here, waiting for the man up there
     I hope the engineer is kind enough to let it take me there

 IV.   Blue railroad train, a good old pal to me
     Gets me where I want to go
     I get transportation free

PRISONER BLUES   Traditional

  1. Just like a prisoner who can't escape
    Your love has bound me to my mistake
    Now that I'm losing you
    And I'm trying to make you care
   Trying to change your mind
    Please don't go away and leave me here

  2. Tears on my pillow, blues on my bed
    I can't stop thinking about the things you said
    Now that I'm losing you
    And I'm trying to make you care

Trying to change your mind
 Please don't go away and leave me here.

3. Just like a prisoner without a key
    Your love has bound me to misery

    Now that I'm losing you
    And I'm trying to make you care
    I'm trying to change your mind
    Please don't go away and leave me here

HEAVY HIPPED WOMAN   Traditional

Quit yo long-time talking bout yo heavy – hipped woman,
She gone gone, oh babe, she done gone
Quit yo long-time talking bout yo heavy-hipped woman
She done gone, oh babe, she done gone

My woman she keep on grumbling
Bout a new pair of shoes, oh, baby, new pair of shoes
My woman she keep on grumbling
Bout a new pair of shoes, oh, baby, new pair of shoes

I give her five dollars, just to buy some tans
She come back whooping and hollering, with a pair of brogans
I give her five dollars, just to buy some tans
She come back whooping and hollering, with a pair of brogans

When I cross that wide old mountain, then Ill be free
That heavy-hipped woman made a fool out of me
When I cross that wide old mountain, then Ill be free
That heavy-hipped woman made a fool out of me

WHO YOU BEEN LOVING (Since I've been gone)
Traditional
Who you been loving since I been gone
Long tall man with a red coat on
Good for nothing baby
Why you doing me wrong

Who you been loving since I been gone
Who you been loving since I been gone

Who's been playing around with you
Long tall man with eyes of blue
Good for nothing baby, why can't you be true

Who you been loving since I been gone
Who you been loving since I been gone

Release: Somebody saw you bout the break of day
              Drinking and dancing in a cabaret
              He was long and tall and had plenty of cash
              He had a red Cadillac and a black mustache

Come on over here let me sing you a song
Who you been loving since I've been gone

BLUES JUMP A RABBIT   Traditional

 G   Emi   G Emi G   Emi Bf
Blues jump up a rabbit he'll run a mile
 G   Ami   Bf;   G   F   G
Oh peace of mind, leave all his troubles behind

Wish I was in cool Colorado on some mountain high
I'd see my darling as he went riding by

Some want white or yellow, some crave black or brown
The one I'm needing wont ever turn me down

Blues jump a rabbit, he'll run a mile, Poor little rabbit, crying

DON'T FOLLOW ME DOWN   Traditional

Don't follow me down
Follow me down to some old backstreet in town
Don't follow me down
Follow me down to some old backstreet in tow

Went to my Momma and got down on my knees, hollering
Oh Momma won't you forgive me, please
Went to my Momma and got down on my knees, hollering
Oh Momma won't you forgive me, please

Nobody down on the street will ever cry for me
Cry for me
Nobody down on the street will ever cry for me
Cry for me

Momma told me, Papa told me too
Living down on the street gonna be the death of you
Momma told me, Papa told me too
Living down on the street gonna be the death of you

OLD RUBIN   (900 MILES)   Traditional

On the first day of the year Old Rubin come up here
And he has never pulled up since that day.
I took my razor blade and laid Old Rubin in the shade
And started a grave-yard of my own

I went down to town and saw the train roll down
Hear the whistle blow 900 miles
If I die a railroad man you can bury me in the sand
So I can hear ol no. 9 as she rolls by

Yonder comes the train and it's numbered no. 9
I'm gonna catch that train and ride the blinds
If this train runs me right I'll see my woman Saturday night
Cause I'm 900 miles from my home

If my woman says no then I'll railroad no more
Sidetrack my train and then come home
Number 9 made a wreck, killed my baby I expect
Hear the brakeman holler oh Lord

There are tears in my eye and I wish that I could die,
I'm trying to read a letter from my home

900 MILES   Traditional

I'm walking down the track, I got tears in my eyes
Trying to read a letter from my home
If this train runs right, I'll be home tomorrow night
Cause I'm 900 miles from my home
And I hate to hear that lonesome whistle blow

I'll pawn you my watch, and I'll pawn you my chain,
Pawn you my gold diamond ring
If this train runs right, I'll be home tomorrow night
Cause I'm 900 miles from my home
And I hate to hear that lonesome whistle blow

This train that I ride on, is a hundred coaches long
You can hear that whistle blow a hundred miles
If this train runs right, I'll be home tomorrow night
Cause I'm 900 miles from my home
And I hate to hear that lonesome whistle blow

MULE SKINNER BLUES   By: Peter & Jimmy Rodgers, George Vaughan

Good morning Cap'n, good morning son
Good morning Cap'n, good morning son
Do you need another mule skinner
Out on your new road line

Well I like to work and I'm roving all the time
Well I like to work and I'm roving all the time
I can carve my initials
On a mules behind

Well it's hey lil water boy, bring that bucket round
Well it's hey lil water boy, bring that bucket round
If you don't like your job,
Let the water bucket down

Well I'm working on my own job, at a dollar and a dime a day
Well I'm working on my own job, at a dollar and a dime a day
I got three woman waiting on a Saturday night
Just to draw my pay

Lord I been working hard and I feel so bad
Lord I been working hard and I feel so bad
I've got a good woman
 and I want to keep her glad

I'm an old mule skinner from down Kentucky way
I'm an old mule skinner from down Kentucky way
I can make any mule listen
Or I won't accept no pay.

SOUTHERN WOMAN BLUES   By: Blind Lemon

Way down south oughtta see them women shimmy and shake
Way down south oughtta see them women shimmy and shake
New way to make a weak man break his knee

You give them greens and boy they can really cook
You give them greens and boy they can really cook
Make a jelly roll got me feeling so good

Down south I love my whiskey good
Down south I love my whiskey good
Then looking at woman makes my blood want to get up

Southern woman boy sure are hard to beat
Southern woman boy sure are hard to beat
So easy to get along with and Lord so quick

I'm going down south I'll believe I'll take my hook
I'm going down south I'll believe I'll take my hook
Gonna try so many women The catch that hasn't been took

Me and my sugar something has gone wrong
Me and my sugar something has gone wrong
I went to go fishing Man I broke my pole

DELIA   By: Blind Blake (Bahamas Blues Singer)

Tony shot his Delia, on a Friday night.
First time that he shot her, she staggered and she died
Delia's gone, One more round
Delia's gone, One more round

Sent for the Doctor, Doctor come too late
Sent for the minister, took her to her fate

Delia's gone, One more round
Delia's gone, One more round

They took Tony's Delia, dressed her all in brown
Took her to the grave-yard, twas there they laid her down
Delia's gone, One more round
Delia's gone, One more round

GO ON BLUES   Traditional: Argmt; Brownie McGhee

You walked off and left me, Cause I was slow getting a break
Now I begin to get lucky, now you see your grave mistake

Chorus: So you go on I got your places filled,
            You can't pull me down,
            I'm climbing to the top of the hill

People all told you I was the dead beat on your hands
Why don't you let him go and get you another man   (Chorus)

I burned all your love letters, I was left without a friend
So I got me a Virginia women that will stick until the end   (Chorus)

You seem to be the type that don't want me to have no friends,
thought when you put me down I wouldn't try it again   (Chorus)

I said I wouldn't tell nobody but the talks all over town

What a fool you was when you put a good man down   (Chorus)

LONESOME BLUES   Traditional: Argmt; Brownie McGhee

I woke up this morning feeling sad and blue
Baby done quit me what am I gonna do?

Chorus: You know I'm lonesome, and the blues all in my way,
(talking to me)
          I may be down now buddy, but I will be up someday

Boys ain't it hard to love another man's girlfriend,
Can't see her when you want to, got to see her when you can
(Chorus)

I got to walk by myself, got to sleep by myself
While the woman I love is loving somebody else   (Chorus)

My baby left me, she left me broken-down
Said goodbye daddy I'll see you in another town   (Chorus)

I wake up some mornings about the break of day,
Reach and get the pillow, where my baby lay   (Chorus)

ORIGINAL TALKING BLUES   Traditional

If you want to get to heaven tell you what to do, got to grease your
feet in mutton stew.
You slide out of the devils hand & ooze right into the promised land.
Take it easy, but go greasy.

Standing in the corner by the mantlepiece, up in the corner by a
bucket of grease,
I stuck my feet in that bucket of grease, went a slipping up & down
the mantelpiece.
Hunting matches, cigarette stubs, left overs.

Down in the holler just a sitting on a log my hand on the trigger & my
eye on a hog.

I pulled that trigger & the gun went zip, & I grabbed that hog with all my grip.
Course I can't eat hog eyes, but I love pork chops.

Don in the hen-house on my knees I though I heard a chicken sneeze,
It was only a rooster saying his prayers giving out thanks to the hens upstairs.
Rooster preaching, hen's singing, little young pullets just sort of doing he best they can.

I was down behind the hen-house the other night, it was awful dark, I didn't have no light,
The farmers dog ran out by chance & he bit a big hole in the seat of my pants.
I jumped a gully, plowed around. Felt funny.

Now I'm just a city dude a living out of town,
everybody knows me as moonshiner Brown,
I make the beer and I drink the slop, got 9 little orphans that call me pop,
I'm patriotic. Raising soldiers. Red cross nurses.

Mama's in the front room a fixing the yeast, daddy's in the bedroom greasing his feet,
Sisters at the back room a squeezing out the hops, brothers at the window just a watching for the cops,
Drinking home brew. Getting drunk.

DEALING WITH THE DEVI Traditional: Argmt; Brownie McGhee

Salt in my gravy, potash in my tea, I know that women trying to poison me.
I told you little women and I'll tell you again, if you don't me find you another man.
Got a shotgun in the corner, rotgut on the bed, wants to catch me sleeping so she can whop my head

Chorus: I been dealing with the devil (3x)
              Women don't love me no more,

One thing bout this woman I don't understand, always got a big stick in her hand.
 I tell you one thing I ain't going by myself, If you don't want me I'll get someone else. - Chorus:

SCREAMING AND CRYING BLUES   (Fuller)

I lay down last night laughing, I woke up this morning screaming and crying
I lay down last night laughing, I woke up this morning screaming and crying
I was worried & grieving about that gal gone off and left me behind.

I said she gone and left me sick on my bed
I said she gone and left me sick on my bed
Said I didn't have nobody to hold my worried head.

I said I don't care where you go mama, I don't care how long you stay
I said I don't care where you go mama, I don't care how long you stay
Have a good time baby bring you back home someday

I BEEN HOODOO   Traditional: Argmt; K. D.

Cosy woman by the railroad track
She burns a candle on her fur sack
 She gives illusion and baking confusion
Just don't know where I'm at

  Chorus: I been hoodoo
          I been hoodoo
          I been hoodoo
          Hoodoo coudoo youdoo
          You burn a candle on me

She dropped the rabbit and burn us
You messed in high but a hangs too low
This miss-turn-road I've got to cross

Three days a bin a running and I'm still lost - Chorus:

Ever since then my leads been bad
my teeth chatter now, what's the matter
I asked the child what it's all about
She give me a dirty look and my hair fell out - Chorus

I THOUGHT I HEARD BB SAY   Traditional; Argmt; (K.D.)

  Chorus: Open up the window let the bad air out
             Open up the window let the bad air out
             I thought I heard him shout:

Nasty it's dirty take it away
Terrible awful, take it away - Chorus

I heard judge Fogarty say
"30 days in the market, take him away,
give him a new broom"   - Chorus:

I heard Frank Doogan shout
Give him the money gal
before I beat it out
like I splained you
Fore I beat it out. - Chorus:

THE WAY I FEEL   Traditional: Argmt; Brownie McGhee

If you've ever been down then you know just how I feel
I feel like an Indian engine Ain't got no driving wheel (X2)

You don't believe I been thinking, Look what a hole I'm in,
You don't believe I love you, Look what a fool I've been (X2)

Nobody cares when I'm crying, nobody cares when I'm all alone,
Nobody cares when I'm living, you can't love me when I'm dead and
gone. (X2)

It's this a-way I feel tell it any place I be,
 That's the only thing will give my poor heart ease. (X2)

You used to be mine, look who's got you now,
Lord sure can't keep you, don't mean no good nohow. (X2)

TRUCKING LITTLE BABY   Traditional

Chorus: She's a trucking lil baby. Goin' tell it everywhere I go (repeat 3 X)

 I got a gal lives across that hill, she's gonna quit me but I love her still.
That there girl she named Marie, she got good jelly but she's stingy with me. - Chorus:

Now wake up boys don't be no fool, here's a lil gal just built for two
She's long and thin she's made so round she can look up long as I can down. - Chorus:

Get out boy and shut your door, I got to truck some before I go.
I tell you boy cause you my pal, mighty bad sign to advertise your gal.   -   Chorus:

COME ON IF YOUR COMIN   Tampa Red

Chorus: Come on if your a-comin or just let me be. (3X)

Now just tell me baby what you gonna do,
I've got tired of waiting around for you. - Chorus:

Why you sitting here evil as any gal can be,
I just got tired of the way your driving me. - Chorus:

You know I love you baby and you know the reason why,
So you better tell me the truth baby, or tell a mighty good lie. - Chorus:

Why you been drinking all nite baby, and here you been drunk all day,
But you better remember baby, every word I say.   - Chorus:

Why you better love me baby, and love me with a thrill,
cause if you don't baby some other woman will.   - Chorus:

WINNSBORO COTTON MILL BLUES   Traditional

Chorus: I got the blues, I got the Winnsboro cotton mill blues,
            Lordy spoolings hard, you know and I know I sure don't
have to tell,
            You work for Tom Watson got to work like hell I got the
blues,
            I got the Winnsboro cotton mill blues.

Old man Sergeant sitting at the desk, the damn fool wouldn't give us
no rest,
He'd take the nickels off a a dead mans eye to buy a coca cola and a
Eskimo pie – Chorus:

When I die don't bury me at all, just hang me up on the spool room
wall.
Place a knitter in my hand, so I can spool in the promised land. -
Chorus:

When I die don't bury me deep, bury me down on 600 street,
Place a bobbin in each hand, so I can dolph in the promised land. -
Chorus:

GOIN HOME BOYS   Traditional
(chain gang)

Chorus: I'm going home boys time won't make me stay,
            My time is over through these chains away.
            I'm going home boys time won't make me stay,
            My time is over through these chains away.

I heard from my momma her letter made me cry,

If she could only see me, I know she'd surely die.   - Chorus:

When they brought me here boys here boys, I lost my brother too,
White folks up and shot him there was nothing I could do. - Chorus

You'll have a train boys, gone up in New York
Leaver this rack pile if I have to ride the rails.   - Cho

SWEET MOMA   Traditional

D   A   F   D   A   D

Sweet baby don't be mean to me
Sweet baby don't be mean to me

I been waiting for you
Such a dog-gone lonesome time
For somebody just like you
To change these blues of mine

Sweet moma don't yo turn me down
Hey sweet moma don't you turn me down
that's why I keep hanging around
don't you treat me mean

I'M LEAVING COLORADO   Traditional

Chorus: I'm leaving Colorado, leaving it behind,
          Every mile I travel there's trouble on my mind

Somewhere up in the canyon,
Somewhere on a mountain high,
It's there I'll return to slumber,
As the wind sings a lullaby.   - Chorus:

Far off in the foothills,
High in the whispering pine,
It's there I left my truelove,
And what little life was mine.   - Chorus

And the blues chase up a rabbit,
Rabbit he looks behind,
He sees the world a-crying,
And he knows no peace of mind   - Chorus:

I SAT DOWN IN A GAMBLING GAME   Traditional
(AND I COULD NOT PLAY MY HAND)

Good morning Mr, Railroad man
What time do your trains go by
"At 9:16 abd 2:44
and 25 minutes till five."

It's 9:16 and 2:44
And 25 minutes ti five
Thank you Mr. Railroad man
I want to watch your trains roll by.

(Danville Girl)

I just sat down in a gamblin' game
And I could not play my hand
Just thinkin' about that woman I love
Run away with another man

Run away with another man, poor boy
Run away with another man, poor boy

I was thinking about that women I love
Run away with another man.

FOLK SONG REPETOIRE

A WALKING AND A TALKING (Old Smokey in minor) traditional

A walking and a talking for pleasure am I
For to see me true willy as he passes by
For to greet him is pleasure, but parting is grief,
And an unconstant lover is worse than a thief

For a thief will but rob you and take what you have
But an unconstant lover will lead you to the grave
And the grave will consume you, and turn you to dust
Not one girl in twenty, a poor boy can trust

Now the cuckoo is a fine bird, he sings as he flies
He never sings cuckoo till the spring of the year

DOWN BY THE RIVERSIDE
Traditional

I'm gonna lay down my atom bomb, Down by the riverside
I'm gonna lay down my atom bomb, Down by the riverside

Chorus: I ain't gonna study war no more
            I ain't gonna study war no more
            I ain't gonna study war no more
            I ain't gonna study war no more
            I ain't gonna study war no more
            I ain't gonna study war no more

I'm gonna talk with the prince of peace, Down by the riverside
I'm gonna talk with the prince of peace, Down by the riverside
(Chorus)

I'm gonna lay down my sword and shield, Down by the riverside
I'm gonna talk with the prince of peace, Down by the riverside
(Chorus)

I'm going to the promised land, Down by the riverside
I'm going to the promised land, Down by the riverside
(Chorus)

EASTER REBELLION, 1916   Traditional

Oh down to the glen I went one morn
To a city there rode I
There Ireland's lines of marching men
In squadrons passing by

No pipe did hum nor battle drum
Did send it straight and true
Nor the angelus bell, nor the living swell
Rang out in the foggy dew

Right proudly high over Dublin town
They hung out the flag of war
For was better to die beneath the Dublin sky
Then at Soreigh or Cullen Bar

And from the plains of Ryoming
Strong men came hurrying through
For Brittania's sons, with their long-range guns
Sailed in through the foggy dew

The bravest fell, and the solemn bell
Banged mournfully and clear
For those that died, that eastern tide
In the springtime of the year.

The world could gaze with deep amaze
At those fearless men but true
Who bore the fight, that freedoms light
Might shine through the foggy dew

I'M A DUST BOWL REFUGEE   Anonymous

I'm a dust bowl refugee
Just a dust bowl refugee
From the dust bowl to the peach bowl
Now the peach bowl is killing me

Cross the mountain to the sea
Come the wife and kids and me
It's a hot dusty highway
For a dust bowl refugee

Lord it's always been that way
Here today and on our way
Down the mountain, cross the desert
Just a dust bowl refugee

We are ramblers so they say
We are only here today
And we travel with the season
We are dust bowl refugees

WALKING IN JERUSULEM   Traditional

Who're those people dressed in red
(Walking in Jerusalem, just like John)
Must be the children that Moses led
(Walking in Jerusalem, just like John)

Chorus: I want to be ready, I want to be ready
         I want to be ready
            (Walking in Jerusalem, just like John)

Who're those people dressed in white
(Walking in Jerusalem, just like John)
Must be the children of the Israelite
(Walking in Jerusalem, just like John)   (Chorus)

If you get to heaven before I do
(Walking in Jerusalem, just like John)
Tell all my brothers I'm coming too

(Walking in Jerusalem, just like John)   (Chorus)

My feet took a walk in the midnight sun
(Walking in Jerusalem, just like John)
Moon and stars were shining through
 (Walking in Jerusalem, just like John)   (Chorus)

MOLLY AND TEMBROOKS   Traditional

Molly was a chestnut mare
With a black and shaggy mane
She ran all around Memphis
Beat the Memphis train

She ran all around Memphis
And beat the Memphis Train

Run Molly Run, Run Molly Run
Tembrooks gonna beat you
To the bright and shining sun

Out in California where Molly done as she please
Come back to old Kentucky gal
Always won with ease

Ain't no horse beat Molly
Same for Tembrooks too
Gonna be a special race
See how they do

Biggest proudest horse race
Country ever seen
Tembrooks is a king for sure
Molly is a queen

Woman are a screaming
Children are a crying
Men are a hollering
And old Tembrooks is dying

Gonna Hitch old Molly
Hitch her in the shade
Gonna bury old Tembrooks
In a coffin ready made

Run Molly run
Run Molly run
Tembrooks gonna beat you
To the bright Morning sun

GOOFUS   Traditional

I was born on a farm out in Ioway
A flaming youth who was bound to fly away
I packed my grip and grabbed my saxophone
Can't read notes, but I play anything by ear
I make up tunes on the sounds I want to hear
When I would play, people would say
Sounds a little Goofus to me

Corn-fed chords appeal to me
I like the rustic harmony
Hold the note and change the key
That's called Goofus
Not according to the rules
That you learn in music schools
But the folks still dance like fools
They go Goofus

Got me a job but I couldn't keep it long
The leader said that I played all the music wrong
So I branched out with an outfit of my own
Got me together a new kind of orchestry
We all played the same Goofus harmony
And I must admit we made a hit
Goofus has been lucky for me

THE MOURNING DOVE   Traditional

Ami – Cmaj – G – C – Ami – G – G

Cold blows the wind, my own true love
And gently drops the rain
I've never had but one true love
And it's brought me only pain.
Down in yonder grove
Where we were used to walk
The fairest flower I ever saw
Is withered to a stalk

The flowers withered and dead sweetheart
And never shall return
And since I lost my own true love
What can I do but mourn

Don't you see that mourning dove
Sitting on yonder tree
Longing for his own true love
As I shall long for thee

THE CABIN ON THE HILL   Traditional

There's a happy child at home
In my memory I can see
Standing out upon a hill
In the shadow of a tree

If I only had my way
It would give my heart a thrill
Just to simply wander backstreet
To the cabin on the hill

Oh, I want to wander back
To the cabin on the hill
Beneath the shadow of a tree
I would like to linger still
Just to be with those I love
It would give my heart a thrill
Just to simply wander back
To the cabin on the hill

But the saddest thought of all
I can nevermore return
To the happy child at home
Matters not at all my tears

But there'll be a better home
Where we all will come and live
In the mansion in the sky
And the stand upon the hill

BAYOU GIRL   Traditional

Daylight comes, sunshine shines
Night is gone, as is John
The Bayou girl she's crying again
What the Bayou girl don't know
What the Bayou girl don't know
What the Bayou girl don't know
John ain't coming back

1st Chorus:
Every single morning without fail
Shes watching everything that floats or sails
Sometimes the Bayou girl takes a pirouge ride
What the bayou girl don't know
What the Bayou girl don't know
What the Bayou girl don't know
The pirouge's tied

She's lived here all her life
she grew up as John's wife
The Bayou girl knows no other world
But the Bayou girl ain't seen
But the Bayou girl ain't seen
But the Bayou girl ain't seen
New Orleans

2nd Chorus
The fat black cat bites, wheres John tonight?

He's in New Orleans, messing with the Cajun queens
And the Bayou girl cries by the river bank
What the Bayou girl don't know
What the Bayou girl don't know
What the Bayou girl don't know
John ain't selling hides
(Repeat first verse)

GREAT SPECKLED BIRD   Traditional: Argmt; K.D

Key: Bf


```
 F                                              D7
You can take a silver dollar and throw it on the ground and it'll
 G7                        C7
Roll because it's round, a woman never knows
                                  F
What a good man she's got until she turns him down
                                      D7
My honey listen, you better listen to me
 G7                           Bf
I want you to understand. As a silver dollar goes
        F       D7      G7            C7      F
From hand to hand a woman  goes, from man to man
```


```
            B6                  E6
Oh what a beautiful thought I am thinking
      F7                      Bf
Concerning the great speckled bird
  Bf7                      Ef
Remember her name is recorded
         F7               B6
On the pages of God's holy word
```


She is spreading her winks for a journey
She's going to leave by and by
When the trumpet shall sound in the morning
She'll rise and go up in the sky.

When he comes descending from heaven
On the cloud as is written in the word
I'll be joyfully carried up to meet him
On the wings of the great speckled bird

DUNCAN AND BRODY   Traditional

Duncan was standing and tending bar
Along came Brody in his electric car
Got a mean look right in his eye
Gonna shoot somebody just to see him die
Been on the job too long

Duncan was standing and tending bar
Along came Brody with his big shining star
Said Brody "Duncan your under arrest"
And Duncan shot a hole right in Brody's chest

Brody you know that you done wrong
Breaking in here with a game going on
Breaking down the windows beating on the doors
Now your lying dead on the barroom floor

Old king Brody was a big fat man
Doctor reached out took a hold of his hand
Felt for his pulse and then he said
I believe to my soul old king Brody's dead

When the women heard that old king Brody was dead
They went back home and re-ragged in red
Comes slipping and sliding walking down the street
In their big mother-hubbards and stocking feet.

THE WIDE MISSOURI   By: G.I.American Army Songs

Oh Shenandoah, I love your daughter
     Away, you rolling river.
Oh, Shenandoah I love your daughter
     Away, I'm bound away,

Cross the wide Missouri.

For seven years I courted Sally,
For seven years she would not have me.

She would not have me for a lover
Because she loved a wagon soldier

She must have had another lover,
Because she had herself a baby.

THE RICH OLD MISER   Traditional

A rich old miser married me,
His age was four score years and three.
Mine was only seventeen.
I wish his face I'd never seen'

No sooner had he got me home,
Then he began to shout and moan.
He beat me and he banged me too,
Til my poor back was black and blue.

Well, early next morning I arose,
And after putting on my clothes,
Before another word was said,
I banged my ladle over his head.

So he began to shout about,
But I was young and strong and stout,
Before he got out from the bed
I banged my ladle over his head.

So all you wives who are going to marry,
Mind what housing things you carry.
Wherever you go, whatever you do,
Always carry a ladle or two.

WHEN I WAS SINGLE   Traditional

When I was single my clothes were the best
Now that I'm Married I'm lucky I'm dressed

Chorus: Ah, but still I'll love you, I'll forgive you,
         I'll be with you wherever you go.

When I was single I wore a black shawl,
Now that I'm married I've nothing at all   - Cho:

When I was single you'd take me to dine
Now you insist there's no cooking like mine. - Cho:

When I was single we'd hug all the night,
Now it's I'm tired, please turn out the light,
Still I love you I'll forgive you
I'll be with you wherever you go

I'TS THE SAME THE WHOLE WORLD OVER   Traditional

It's the same the whole world over
It's the poor what gets the blame
While the rich get all the pleasure
ain't it a blooming shame.

She was just a parson's daughter
Pure, unstained was her name
Til a country squire came courting,
And the poor girl lost her name.

Chorus: It's the same the whole world over
           It's the poor what gets the blame
           While the rich get all the pleasure
           ain't it a blooming shame.

See him with his hounds and horses,
Drinking champagne in his club,
While the victim of his passion
Drinks guiness in the pub.   - Chorus:

There came a wealthy landlord,
Marriage was the tale he told,
There was no one else to take her,
So she sold herself for gold.   - Chorus

In a cottage down in Sussex,
There her grieving parents live,
Drinking champagne that she sends them,
But not willing to forgive.   - Chorus:

DUNDERBECKE   Traditional

There was a man named Dunderbecke, invented a machine,
for grinding things to sausage meat, and it was run by steam.
Now kitchen cats and long-tailed rats will never more be seen.
They'll all be ground to sausage meat in Dunderbecke's machine.

Chorus:
Oh Dunderbecke, oh Dunderbecke, how could you be so mean For
ever having invented the sausage meat machine

Now kitchen cats and long-tailed rats will never more be seen.
They'll all be ground to sausage meat in Dunderbeck's machine.

One day a little boy walked in to Dunderbecke's store
A little piece of sausage meat was lying on the floor
While the boy was waiting he whistled up a tune.
The sausage meat got up and barked and ran around the room.   -
Chorus:

One morning something, it went wrong, the machine, it wouldn't go.
So Dunderbecke, he stopped inside, the reason for to know.
His wife she had a nightmare, she was walking in her sleep.
She gave a yank, and turned the crank, and Dunderbecke was meat -
Chorus:

FOLOW WASHINGTON   Traditional

The day is broke, my boys, push on and follow, follow Washington.
'Tis he that leads the way, my boys, tis he that leads the way

Where he commands, we will obey, through rain or snow by night
and day,
Determined to be free my lads until our cause prevails

With heart and hand, and God our trust, we'll freely fight our cause is
just.
Push on, my boys! My boys, push on, follow Washington

Til freedom reigns, our hearty band will fight like true Americans,
March on, my lads! My lads march on, follow Washington

The day is broke, my boys, push on and follow, follow Washington.
Tis he that leads the way, my boys, tis he that leads the way.

THE HORNET AND THE PEACOCK   Traditional

The Peacock was bred in the land of King George,
Her feathers were fine and her tail very large,
She spread herself forth like a ship in full sail
And prided herself on the size of her tail.

> Chorus: Sing hubber and bubber cries old Granny Weal,
> The Hornet can tickle the British bird's tail.
> Her stings, they are sharp and they'll sting without fail,
> Bad cess to the British cries old Granny Weal

Away flew this bird at the word of command,
Her flight was directed to freedom's own land,

The Hornet discovered the ship on the sail
And quickly determined to tickle her tail   - Chorus:

The Peacock then mortally under her wink
Did feel the full force of the Hornets sharp sting,
She flatten her crest like a shoal on a whale,
Sunk by her side and she lowered her tail.   - Chorus

Here's success to brave Lawrence who well knew the nest,
Where the the Hornet with honor and dignity rests,
American Insects, quoth he, I'll be bail,
Will humble King George, til he takes in his tail.   - Chorus

THE JOLLY WAGONER   Traditional

When first I went a-wagoning, a-wagoning I did go
I filled my parents heart with grief, with sorrow, care and woe
And many are the hardships that I have since gone through -ough -
ough,

  Chorus: Sing wo, my lads, sing wo! Drive on my lads, heigh ho!
         Who would not lead the merry life the jolly wagoners do!

Upon a cold and stormy night when wetted to the skin
I bear it with contented heart until I reach the Inn
And there I sit a drinking with the landlord and his kin --in --in. -
Chorus:

Soon Michaelmas is coming on and pleasure we shall find.
We'll make the gold to fly, my boys, like chaff before the wind,
And every lad will love has lass, and she'll respond in kind—ind--ind
- Chorus:

GYPSY DAVY   Traditional

There were three gypsies a-come to my door,

And downstairs ran the lady – O.
One sang high and the other sang low,
And the third one sang bony Biscay – O.

So she pulled on her leather stockings,
Took of her stockings of silken - O.
The bonny bonny clothes lay about her door,
She was gone with the wraggle taggle gypsies – O.

It was late last night when the lord came home,
He was inquiring for his lady -O.
The servants said on every hand,
She's gone with the wraggle-taggle gypsies – O.

Then he got on his bright broiwn steed,
He put on his saddle of leather -O.
And o'er he rode through hill and dale,
Til he came to the camp of the gypsies – O

Oh, would you leave your house and land?
Would you leave your babies – O?
Would you leave your white, white sheets
For the arms of the gypsy Davy ?

What do I care for my home and land?
What do I care for my children – O?
Tonight I'll sleep on the cold, cold ground
In the arms of my gypsy Davy – O!

There were three gypsies a-come to my door,
And downstairs ran the the lady – O.
One sang high and the other sang low,
And the third sang bonny bo0nny Biscay – O.

THE CONESTOGA CURSE   Traditional

Come all you gallant wagoners and turn out man for man,
That;s opposed to the railroads and any such a plan.
It was once we made our money by driving round the team,
But now they are sending all their goods by water or by steam.

If we go to Philadelphia and inquire for a load,
They tell to us directly that it's going by the railroad.
The rail-men and the canawlers may this plan of theirs admire,
But it ruins us poor wagoners and makes your taxes higher.
It ruins wheel-rights, blacksmiths, carters, and every other trade,
So damned to to all the railroads that ever yet was made.
May the devil take the party that invented such a plan,
It'll ruin us poor wagoners and every other man.

The ships they will be coming here with Irish men in loads.
Allk with their picks and shovels to work on the railroads.
And when they settle down to work, it's then we will be fixed,
And they;ll fight us like the devil with their cudgels and their bricks.

The Conestoga wagoners with safety cannot pass,
They blacken both his eyes for just one word of Yankee sass.
If it wasn't for the torment, I'd as lief be down in hell,
As upon the cursed railroad, or the damned canal

So come all ye hardy wagoners and marr5y wealthy wives,
Go find yourself a quiet farm and settle for your lives,
When the corn is all cribbed up and all the grain is safely sowed,
You can sit beside the fireplace and curse the damned railroad.

HARD ROAD TO TRAVEL   Traditional

Well I ain't goin down that big road by myself   (2X)
If I can't take you with me, I'm gonna take somebody else.

We're long and dreary, Lord, and the road is mighty rough (2X)
Seems like the harder and further I travel things get might tough

Well I'd rather be walking, don't appreciate no ride (2X)
Cause the one I love and want, he's not by my side.

I CAME TO THIS COUNTRY IN 1865   Traditional (Lomax)

I came to this country boys, in eighteen sixty-five,
I thought I was most lucky to find myself alive;
I harnessed up my horses, my business to pursue,
I went to hauling coal like I used to do.

The alehouse doors was open, boys, the liquor running free,
Ask soon as one glass emptied, another filled for me;
Instead of hauling six loads, I did not haul but four,
I got so darned drunk, boys, that I couldn't hold no more.

I finished up my supper and went out to the barn,
I saddled up the old gray mare, not meaning any harm,
I rode to the gate and passed the flower mill,
I hardly knew a thing till I come to Watson's Hill.

Now come ald you old women that carries the news about,
Say nothing about us, your bad enough without,
Likewise you old women that likes to make a fuss,
Oh, you're just as bad as we are, perhaps a darn sight worse

THE KINKAIDERS   (tune: :Maryland, My Maryland)

You ask what place I like the best,
The sand hills, the old sand hills;
The place Kinkaiders make their home,
and prairie chickens freely roam
                Chorus: In all Nebraska's wide domain
                        The place we long to see again;
                        The sand hills are the very best,
                        She is the queen of all the rest.
The corn we raise to our delight,
The melons, too, are out of sight.
Potatoes, they are extremely fine,
And can't be beat in any clime. - (Chorus:)

The peaceful cows in pastures dream
And furnish us with golden cream,
So I shall keep my Kinkaid home
 And never shall I roam   -   (Chorus)

TICKLE GROVE POND   Traditional (Alan Mills)

In cutting and in hauling in frost and in snow
We're up against troubles that few people know
and only by patience with courage and grit
And eating plane food can we keep ourselves fit.

The hare and the easy, we take as it comes
And when the ponds freeze over we shorten our runs
To hurry my hauling, the spring coming on
Neaer lost my mare on the Tickle Grove Pond.

      Chorus: Oh, lay hold, William Oldford, lay hold William White!
              Lay hold of the cordage and pull all your might
              Lay hold of the bowline and pull all you can
              And give me a hand with poor kit on the pond

I knew that the ice became weaker each day,
But still took the risk and kept hauling away.
And one icy evening bound home with a load
The mare shoved some halting against the ice road.
Allk this I ignored with a whip handle blow
for man is too stupid dumb creatures to know.
The very next minute the pond gave a sigh
And down to our necks went poor Kitty and I.   -   (Chorus:)

I raised an alarm you could hear for a mile
And neighbors turned up in a very short while. You can always rely
on the Oldsfords and Whites
To render assistance in all your bad plights.
When the bowline was fastened around the mare's breast
William White for a shanty song made a request,
There was no time for thinking, no time for delay,
so straight from my head come this song right away.   - (Chorus)

BUFALO GALS   Traditional

Chorus: As I was walking down the street, down the street, down the
street

A pretty little girl I chanced to meet & we danced by the light of the moon.

I danced with a girl with a hole in her stocking and her hell kept a knocking and her toe kept a rocking. Chorus:

I danced with a gal with a wooden leg, I guess that's the reason they call her Peg.
Chorus:

We're gonna have pork & we're gonna have mutton, If you don't come early you won't get nothing. Chorus

OLD DOLORES   Traditional

In the valley down below, where the little pinions grow,
And it's never less then half a day to water,
There used to be a town where the crick come tumbling down
From a mesa where it never really ought to.

   The night was bright with candlelight,
   The whole town joined the chorus,
    And most any man in sight let his cattle drift at night
    Just to mosey through the streets of Old Dolores.

And things would kind of spin 'til the sun come up again,
Like the back of some old yaller prairie wagon,
And showed up dim and red about half a hundred head
of our saddle ponies standing reins a-dragging.

   The red brick walls and waterfalls,
   Why, the whole world lay before us.
    But the dobie huts are gone, and the goat bells in the dawn
    Don't tinkle in the streets of old Delores.

And the girls from Mexico used to wander to and fro',
There was one; I used to meet by a willow.
But I guess that any girl would give a feller's head a whirl
When the sames been using saddles for a pillow.
   The big cigars and wide-eyed stars,

The friends that waited for us...
If there's any little well inside the gates of Hell
I'll bet the boys have named it Old Dolores.

TRAVELING SHOES Dmaj 6/8   Traditional

Too many people too many times
Keep complaining too much about their troubled minds
So many people itching to speak
Very few practicing anything they;re preaching.

Chorus: Traveling shoes, traveling blues
          Can't seem to lose my weary blues
          Go get my traveling shoes.

Some folks are saying they know me quite well
Some people saying my souls gone to hell
Of them that do and them that don't
there's a few left that will and some that wont

THE HORSE NAMED BILL (Tune: Dixie)   Traditional

I had a horse and his name was Bill,
And when he ran he couldn't stand still.
He ran away – one day –
And also I ran with him

He ran so fast he could not stop
He ran into the barber shop
And fell – Exhaustionized –
His teeth in the barber's left shoulder.

Say I had a gal and her name was Daisy
And when she sang the cat went crazy,
With deliriums – St Vituses   –
and all kinds of cataleptics,

I'm going out in the woods next year
And hunt for bear and not for deer,
I am --- I am not –
I'm a great sharpshootress.

At shooting birds I am a beaut.
There is no bird I cannot shoot,
In the eye, in the ear, in the tooth,
In the fingers.

In 'Frisco bay there lives a whale.
She eats pork-chops by the bale,
By the hatbox,by the hogshead, by the pillbox,
By the schooner.

Her name is Lena, she's a peach,
But don't leave food within her reach,
Or babies, or nursemaids,
Or chocolate ice cream sodas.

I once went up in a balloon so big,
The people on earth, they looked like a pig
Like a mice, like flies, like katy-dids,
Like katy-didn'ts

Well what do you do in a case like that/
What could you do but stamp on your hat,
On your toothbrush, on your toothpaste,
And anything that's helpless?

THE OLD SOLDIERS OF THE KING
Traditional

Since you all must have singing and you won't be said Nay,
I cannot refuse you when you beg and you pray,
So I"ll sing you a song as a poet might say,
Of King George's soldiers when they ran away.
We're the old soldiers of the King and the Kings own regulars .

At Prestonpans we met with the rebels one day.
We marshaled ourselves all in comely array.
Our hearts bid as stand and our heads bid us stay,
But our feet were strong-minded and took us away.
We're the old soldiers of the King and the Kings own regulars .

To Monongahela with fifes and with drums,
Wek marched in fine order with cannons and bombs.
This great expedition cost infinite sums,
But some underpaid doodles, they cut us to crumbs.
We're the old soldiers of the King and the Kings own regulars.

Oh they fought us so unfairly from back of the trees,
If they'd only fight open, we'd have beat them with ease.
They can fight one another that way if they please,
But we won't stand and battle such rascals as they are.
We're the old soldiers of the King and the Kings own regulars .

Yes we turned and we ran, but that shouldn't disgrace us
We did it to prove that the foe could not face us.
And they've little to brag off that's a very plain case.
Though we've lost in the fight, we came first in the race.
We're the old soldiers of the King and the Kings own regulars .

DARK AS A DUNGEON   Traditional

Come all you young fellows so young and so fine, seek not your
fortune way down in the mines.
It will form like a habit and seep in your soul till the streams of your
blood runs as black as the coal.

Chorus: Its dark as a dungeon & damp as the dew the dangers are
doubled & the pleasures are few,
Where the rain never falls and the sun never shines, It's dark as a
dungeon way down in the mines.

There's many a man I've seen in my day, who lived just to labor his
whole live away.
Like a fiend with his dope or a drunkard his wine, a man will have
lust for the lure of the mines Cho:

I hope when I'm dead and the ages shall roll, my body will blacken
and turn into coal,
Then I'll look from the door of my heavenly home, and pity the
miners a digging my bones, Cho:

THE ROVING GAMBLER   Traditional

I am a roving gambler
I've gambled up and down,
Whenever I meet with a deck of cards,,
I lay my money down.   (repeat twice)

Oh, the doctor leads a happy live,
The lawyer he does well,
But the love I bear for the deck of cards
No human heart can tell.   (repeat twice)

I wouldn't be a farmer,
He's always in the rain.
I just want to be a gambling man,
]And wear a big gold chain,   (repeat twice)

I hadn't been to New York town,
But two hours of three,
When I fell in love with a pretty little gal,
And she fell in love with me.   (repeat twice)

She took me to her parlor,
she cooled me with her fan.
She whispered soft in her mother's ear,
"I love a gambling man." (repeat twice)

"Oh mother, Oh dear mother,
Forgive me if you can.
But if you ever see me back again
It'll be with a gambling man."   (repeat twice)

ROCK ABOUT MY SARO JANE   Traditional

Chorus: Rock about my Saro Jane, Rock about my Saro Jane.
              Oh there's nothing to do but to set down and sing,
              And rock about my Saro Jane.

I've got a wife and five little children, I believe we;ll take a ride on the
big Macmilan - Cho:

Biler is busted & the whistle done blowed, the head captain done fell
overboard   -   Cho :

Engine gave a crack and the whistle gives a squall, engineers gone to
a hole in the wall - Cho:

Yankees build boats for to shoot them rebels, my muskets loaded and
I'm gonna hold her level. - Cho:

CAN'T YOU DANCE THE POLKA!   Traditional

Now, shipmates, if you'll listen to me, I'll tell to you in my song,
Of things that happened to me when I came home from Hong Kong.
        Chorus: To me way, you Santy, my dear Annie,
                    Oh, you New York girls, can't you dance the polka!

As I walked down through Chatham Street, a fair maid did I meet,
Who kindly asked me to see her home she lived on Bleeker Street -
Chorus:

"Now if you come with me, you can have a treat,
You can have a glass of brandy, dear, and something nice to eat."   -
Chorus:

When we got up to Bleeker Street we stopped at forty-four,
Her so-called mother and sister was a-standing at the door.   -
Chorus:

And when we got inside the house the drinks was passed around,

The liquor was so doggone strong my head went round and round. -
Chorus:

When I awoke next morning I had an aching head,
I found myself there all alone, stark naked on the bed.   -
Chorus:

My gold watch and my pocketbook and lady friend were gone.
With a barrel for a suit of clothes, I signed up for Cape Horn.   -
Chorus:

BRAVE WOLFE   Traditional

Bad news has come to town, bad news is carried. Some say my love
is dead, some say he's married
As I was pondering on this I took to weeping. They stole my love
away whilst I was sleeping.
I'll go and tell my love that I will never leave her, All in the wars in
France I'm bound forever
All in the wars of France where the cannon does rattle, there I'll
myself advance and face the battle,

Love here's a ring of gold long years I've kept it. Madame it's for
your sake will you accept it?

When you the posy read, think on the giver, Madam remember me,
I'm undone forever.
Then away went this brave youth & embarked upon the ocean, to free
Amerikay as his intentions.
He landed in Quebec with all his party, the city to attack, being brave
and hearty.

He drew his army up in the lines so pretty, on the plains of Abraham,
back of the city,
At a distance from the town, where the French would meet him.
In double numbers there resolved to beat him

Montcalm & this brave youth together walked, between 2 armies they
like brothers talked,

Till each one took his post and did retire, It was then these numerous hosts commenced their fire.

Little did he think that death was so near him, Yes little did he think that death was so near him.
When shot down from his horse was this our hero, we'll long lament our loss in tears of sorrow.

He raised up his head where the cannons did rattle & to his aide he said 'how goes the battle?"
His aide replied "it's ended in our favor then says this brave youth "I quit this earth with pleasure."

(Repeat first verse)

THE SQUID JIGGING GROUND   Traditional

Oh, this is the place where the fisherman gather
With oilskins, boots, and Cape Ann;s battened down.
All sizes and figures, with squid lines and jiggers,
They congregate here on the squid jigging ground

Some are working their jiggers while others are yarning,
Some standing up but there's more lying down,
While all sorts of fun, tricks and jokes are begun,
They wait for the squid on the squid jigging ground.

Now the man with the whiskers is old Jacob Steele,
He's getting well up but he's still pretty sound,
While uncle Bob Hoskins wears six pair of stockings
Whenever he's out on the squid jigging ground.

Oh there's a man from the Harbor and a man from the Tickle,
All kinds of motor boats, gray, green and brown,
Then – Hey! Whats the row? Why, he's jigging one now!
The very first squid on the squid jigging ground.

Holy smoke what a scuffle! All hands are excited!
It's a wonder to me there is nobody drowned.
Confusion and bustle and wonderful hustle!

They're all jigging squids on the squid jigging ground.

There's some of them jigging while others is ducking,
Spots of the squid juice is flying around.
Oh, one poor boy got it right in the eye,
But they don't give a damn on the squid jigging ground.

So if you should ever incline to go squidding,
Just leave your white shirt and collar in town.
Or if you get cranky without a silk hanky,
Better stay clear of the squid jigging ground.

GROUND HOG   Traditional Argmt K.D.

One old woman was the mother of us all
One old woman was the mother of us all
She fed us on ground hogs
Soon as we could crawl.

Blow your horn and call your dog
Blow your horn and call your dog
We'll go to the woods to catch a groundhog

Skin out the meat and save the hide
Skin out the meat and save the hide
Best damn shoestrings you ever tied

WISE BOY   Argmt: K.D.

"How old do you think I am"
Said the sky to the little boy
I bet your as old as the velvet in
My mama's box tick tocks a broken watch
It's wrapped around musty and soft and proud

I bet your as old as the land of Oz
lunch boxes on trees and
Tik – tok you wind up again my friend
The sky, you and I

But your tiny baby sister
Immortal wonder born of thunder the smallest
Tear shed 1000 years from her eyes on the life of a sky

Ah, younger am! Than the baby
Billy goat crying for his long lost mama
Baby billy goats gotta weather the storm
Till tomorrow

Well this tree on the edge of the meadow
So old it's gotta be hundreds of years
I bet the clouds are older
Said the sky I know

Such a wise little boy and a sweet soul
With beauty like you I'll never be old
The ancient ones long ago foretold
One day together we'll dance with joy

Blue and white on the horizon
Stars are in my blood stream
Such a sweet lil' soul and a wise boy
The ancient ones long ago foretold

One day together, we'll dance with joy
violet and twilight on the threshold
of day and night turquoise and gold
Where no one ever grows old
and we all sing to our hearts delight
about what could happen tonight.

THE FROG IN THE SPRING   Traditional

There once was a frog and he lived in a spring
    Sing song Kitty ketcha kimeo
He was so fat tht he could not sing
    Sing song Kitty ketcha kimeo

    Makeemio, makimee

Madeerio, maware,
Mahigh, mahay
Ma-in come Sally single
Sometime pennywinkle
Income midgecat,
Hittem with a brickbat,
Sing song Kitty ketcha kimeo

Now, way down yonder at the bottom of the creek
the men, they grow to eleven feet   -   Chorus:

They try to sleep but it isn't any use,
Their feet stick out for the hens to roost. - Chorus:

I once had a horse and his name was 'Bill
When he ran he couldn't stand still   -   Chorus

Sing Song Kitty ketch kimeo.

IVE BEEN WANDERING   Traditional

I've been wandering, early and late,
From New York City to the Golden Gate
And it looks like
I ain't never gonna cease my wandering.

I've been working in the army, I've been working on a farm,
And all I've got to show for it is the muscle in my arm,
And it looks like
I ain't never gonna cease my wandering.

There's ducks in the millpond and there's fish in the sea,
It took a re-headed woman to make a fool out of me.
And it looks like
I ain't never gonna cease my wandering.

I worked in the city, I worked in the town
My arms are all worn from the elbows on down

And it looks like
I ain't never gonna cease my wandering.

THE DRUNKARD SON (From the Alabama collection of Lena Hill)

I saw a man at early dawn,
A-standing in the grog-shop door;
His lips were parched and his cheeks had sank,
And I viewed him o'er and o'er   (repeat last two lines)

He rose and to the grog shop went,
Where he had been before
And in a faltering voice he cried
"Oh give me one glass more"   (repeat last two lines)

The host obeyed at his command,
And filled the sparkling bowl,
Saying, "Drink while wife and child do starve,
And ruin your poor soul."   (repeat last two lines)

One year ago I passed that way.
A crowd stood round the rood.
I asked the cause and one replied,
"The drunkard is no more"   (repeat last two lines)

TEMPERANCE SONG   (Curtis Song Collection, NY Folklore
Quarterly – winter 1953)
Forty casks of liquid woe –
     Who'll buy? Who'll buy?
Murder by the gallon, oh,
     Who'll buy? Who'll buy?

Larceny and theft made thin,
Beggary and death thrown in,
Packages of liquid sin –
     Who'll buy? Who'll buy?

Foreign deaths imported pure –
     Who'll buy? Who'll buy?

Warranted not slow but sure –
    Who'll buy? Who'll buy?
Empty pockets by the cask,

Tangled brains by pinted flask,
Vice of any kind you ask –
    Who'll buy? Who'll buy?
Competition we defy –
    Who'll buy? Who'll buy?
Barrels full of pure soul-dye –
    Who'll buy? Who'll buy?
Dye to make the soul jet-black
Dye to make the conscience slack,
Nothing vile do our casks lack –
    Who'll buy? Who'll buy?

THE WEE COOPER O' FIFE
Traditional

Now, there was a young cooper wa' lived i' Fife,
Nickety, nackety, noo noo noo.
He has taken a gentle wife,
Hew, willy wallity, none of your quality,
Nickety, nackety, noo noo noo

She couldna bake, she wouldna brew,
for spoilng all her comely hue.

She wouldna card, she wouldna spin,
For shaming all her gentle kin.

Now, the cooper has gone to his wee shack,
He took a sheepskin across his wifes back.

"Oh, I wouldna thrast ye for your gentle kin,
But I will thrash m' ain sheepskin.

Now, you w' have married a gentle wife,
Nickety, nackety, noo noo noo

Pay you a mind to the coopers wife,
With his: Hey, willy wallity, none of your quality
Nickety, nackety, noo noo noo

THE COWBOYS LAMENT   Traditional

A cowboys life is a mighty dreary life,
some think it's free from care
Rounding up the dogies from morning until night,
Beside of the prarie so bare.

Now, the wolves and the owls with their terrifying howls
Disturb our midnight dreams,
Lying on our slickers in the cold dreary night,
Beside of the Peco's stream.

It's half past four and the noisy cook will roar,
"Get up, It's almost day!"

Slowly we arise and rub our tired eyes,
The sweet sleep of night passed away.

You may talk of your farms or the city's wild alarms,
Or the dangers of sailing on the foam.
Take a cowboy's advice and get a wealthy wife,
And never leave your home.

THE SHEEP SHEARING   Traditional

How delightful to see,
In those evenings in the spring,
The sheep going home to the fold.
The master doth sing,
As he views everything,

And his dog goes before him when told,
And his dog goes before him when told.

The sixth month of the year,

In the month they call June,
When the weathers too hot to be borne,
The master doth say,
As he goes on his way;
"Tomorrow my sheep shall be shorn,
"Tomorrow my sheep shall be shorn."

Now the sheep they're all shorn,
And the wool homeward borne,
Here's a health to our master and flock;
And if we should stay,
Till the last goes away,
I'm afraid it will be past twelve o'clock
I'm afraid it will be past twelve o'clock.

GANDY DANCERS BALL   Traditional

A gandy dancer is a railroad man, and his work is never done
With his pick and his shovel and his willing hand he makes the
railroad run.
There's Mackinaw Mac and Toledo Jack, and the boys from Idaho,
And the Frisco Kid, and Saginaw Sid, and good old cotton-eyed Joe.

Chorus: Oh, they dance on the ceiling, and they dance on the wall
            Swing around, swing around, swing around the jimmy-john
            Swing the pretty girl around the Jimmy, Jimmy, John

The boys will gather to the great affair, the gandy dancers ball
Kissing their ladies with the perfumed hair, and prancing round the
hall
They got the biggest band in all the land and the rhythm rocks the
room,
And they holler out with a mighty shout when the big bass drum goes
boom. - Chorus:

The railroads bring em to the great affair, the gandy dancers ball,
And every land is represented there, the big one's and the small
There's MKT and the old SP and the Lehigh Valley too,
The CNJ and the Santa Fe, the S
Southern and the Soo

ALL MY TRIALS   Traditional

Had a little book was given to me,
And every leaf spelled victory

Chorus: Too late my brothers, too late but never mind
              All my trials Lord, soon be over

If religion was a thing that money could buy
Then the Rich would live and the poor would die

Chorus: Too late my brothers, too late but never mind
              All my trials Lord, soon be over

SWEET SUNNY SOUTH   Traditional

Take me back to the place where I first seen the light
To the sweet sunny south take me home
Whee the mockingbirds sing me to sleep every night
Oh why was I tempted to roam

Take me back let me see what is left that I know
Can it be that the old home is gone
And friends of my childhood indeed must be free
And I must face death all alone

But yet I'll return to the place of my birth
For my Moma is buried nearby
among these green hills I will stay to my death
And lie there at peace when I die

Take me back to the place where the orange trees grow
To my plot neath the evergreen shade
Where flowers from river's green margins did flow
and spread their sweet scent through the glade

OTHER PEOPLES SONGS

IN MY SKIN   Louis Armstrong

Old empty bed
Springs hard as lead
Feels like old Ned
Wish I was dead

No joy for me
No company
Even the mouse
Ran from my house

I'm white inside
But that don't help my case
Cause I can't hide
The color of my face

How will it end
Ain't got a friend
My only sin is
In my skin

GOING DOWN SLOW   Champion Jack DuPree

I have had my fun if I don't get well no more
I have had my fun if I don't get well no more
Because my health is failing me
And I'm going down slow

Write my mother and tell her the shape I'm in
Write my mother and tell her the shape I'm in
Tell here to pray for me
God forgive all my sins

On the next train south you can see me coming home
On the next train south you can see me coming home
 And if you don't see my body
Ain't no use for you to mourn

Tell my mother don't worry. This is all in my prayer
 Just say your child is gone, out in the world somewhere

I SAW YOU   Jefferson Airplane

The summer had inhaled and held it's breath too long
And winter looked the same as if it had never gone
Through an open window with no curtains on
I saw you, I saw you coming back to me

Chorus:
You can't stay and live my way
Scatter my love like leaves in the wind
You always say you want to go away
But I know that it always has been

One begins to read between the pages of a look
The shape of sleepy music and suddenly your hooked
Through the rain upon the trees, the kisses on the run
I saw you – Chorus:

Strolling the hills,traveling the shore
I realize that I've been here before
The shadow in the mist could have been anyone
I saw you   - Chorus:

SOMEONE TO TALK MY TROUBLES TO   Kingston Trio

Sometimes I don't know what to say
Sometimes I don't know what to do
Someone to tell my troubles to

I remember when you were looking down at me
like there was nothing else you'd want to see

Now I'm getting older and I think of all I've done
And I can remember good times so I think of days to come
Somewhere I know someone's waiting for me
Might not be all I want him to be

Someone to talk my troubles to

NORTHERN SONG   George Harrison

If your listening to this song
You may think the chords are going wrong
But they're not; He wrote it just like that

It doesn't matter what chords I play
What words I say or time of day it is
As it's only a northern song

It doesn't really matter what clothes I wear
Or how I fare or if my hair is brown
When it's only a northern son

When you're listening late at night
You may think that the band are not quite right
But they are they just play it like that

It doesn't really matter what chords I play

What words I say or what time of day it is
As it's only a northern song

It doesn't really matter what chords clothes I wear
Or how I fare or if my hair is brown
When it's only a northern song

If you think the harmony
I a little dark and out of key
Your correct, there's nobody there.

It doesn't really matter what chords I play

What words I say or what time of day it is
And I told you there's no one there

LOOK WHAT YOU HAVE DONE   Marshall Crenshaw

    I. Look what you've done, you've made a fool out of me
      Who thought love was true and found out that you
      Were just having fun
      Oh why do you make me blue
      After all I've been good to you

    II. I recall the time you needed somebody and I made you mine
      You needed a friend and I took you in
      And treated you kind
      Oh why do you want to make me blue
      After all I've been good to you
Bridge: I've always been around and I never let you down
      Now you're telling me that you must go
      You know that you're hurting me so

    III.But they'll come a time when your gonna find
      On bended knee your gonna be crying
      Oh believe me when I say it's true
      After all I've been good to you.

NATURE BOY   Nat King Cole

There was a boy
A very strange enchanted boy
They say he wandered very far, very far
Over land and sea
 A little shy
And Sad of Eye
But very wise was he.
And then one day
One magic day he passed my way
And while we spoke of many things, fools and kings,

This he said to me:
The greatest thing you'll ever learn
 Is just to love
And be loved in return

WINDING ROAD   Paul McCartney

The long and winding road that leads to your door
Will never disappear, I've seen that road before
It always lead me here, lead me to your door

The wild and windy night that the rain washed away
has left a pool of tears crying for the day
While weeping, waiting here, let me know the way

Many times I've been alone, and many times I've cried
But still they lead me back to the long winding road
You left me standing here a long time ago
Don't leave me waiting here, lead me to your door

LOVE SONG   Unknown

The singer strings a chord, and bends
The silent after-drum
Into the singularity of my mind

Lover of tears crying pulled-away loss
Lover of music hearing silence between pulse
Lover of fear, shuddering out flung arms
Where we lay naked side by side in the night and did not love.

Outside all I am other, and not mine,
Poured out sweetly in some careless moment.
Endures the inch-long journey into space,
And breaks the tie between birth and eternity
Pain grown strong in my strong pain plucks at my heart
That cherry of a summer tree.

Bird wings know the wind goes

And sing the rock grass water woods to instrument my ears, my tongue
Blossoms bell clapper for a flower
Blown on sweet breathed bone-whistle wind

In reflection the singer seeks only his own eyes, reaching away memories,
The whale buoyant, curving suspended
Huge flesh of life, breathing begin and stop,
First and done.

Light rocks in the water, the moon pulls deep
The whale sings heart and breath
The tides song inside all changeless
bubble beads along a reed

The singer strings a song
Some window reflecting in my eyes, opens.

A feather flight, dream-floating my heart away
Hanged in space, a white cloud
Torn on winds of bird-wings.

I AIN'T NOTHING BUT A DREAM   By: Jerry Merrick

Let the river rock you like a cradle
Climb to the treetops, child if your able
And our hands tie a knot across the table
Come, and touch the things you cannot feel
And close your fingers and fly where I can't hold you

If all the things you feel ain't what they seem
Then don't mind me cause I
Ain't nothing but a dream

The mockingbird sings each separate song
Each song has wings and won't stay long
Do those who hear think he's doing wrong
While the church bell tolls it's one note song

And the school bell is talking to the throng

Come here where your love cannot hear
And close your ears child and listen to what I'll tell you
Follow in the darkest night the songs that may impel you
And the song that I am singing may disturb or serve
to quell you

If all the songs you hear aren't what they seem
Then don't mind me cause
I ain't nothing but a dream

The sun and moon both are right
And we'll see them soon thru days and nights
But silver leaves are mirrors of delight
And the color of your eyes is fiery bright
While darkness blinds the sky with all it's light

Come see where your eyes cannot see
And close you eyes child and look at what I'll show you
Let your mind go reeling out and let the breeze blow you
And maybe when we meet suddenly Ill know you

If all the things you see aren't what they seem
then don't mind me cause
I ain't nothing but a dream
 and you can follow, and,
I ain't nothing but a dream-floating

IF I'D NEVER MET YOU   By: Kitty Wells

I make all the honky tonks
and taverns
Just to see who's hanging around
There I try and drown my sorrows
Just because you let me down

Last night while dancing with another
And gazing in his eyes so blue

I knew I could have loved him
If I never had met you

I can find someone to kiss me
I can find someone to care
But when I need someone
To truly love me
Your not easy to forget

Last night while dancing with another
And gazing in his eyes so blue
I knew I could have loved him
If I never had met you

STRANGE FRUIT   Billie Holiday

Southern trees bear strange fruit
Blood on the leaves and blood at the root
Black bodies swinging in the southern breeze
Strange fruit hanging from the poplar trees

ohhhhhhhh ---   ohhhhhh ----

Pastoral scenes of the gallant south
Of the bulging eyes and twisted mouth
Scent of magnolia sweet and fresh
And the sudden smell of burning flesh

Here is a fruit for the crows to pluck
For the rains to gather, and the wind to suck
For the sun to rot, for the trees to drop,

Ah, here is a strange and bitter crop.
Here is a strange and bitter fruit.

GOT NO HOME IN THIS WORLD   Woody Guthrie

Chorus: I ain't got no home I'm just ramblin round,
         I'm just a wandering working, I go from town to town

Police make it hard, wherever I go
And I ain't go no home in this world anymore

My brothers and my sisters are stranded on this road
It's a hot and dusty road, that a million feet have trod,
Rich man took my house and he drove me from my door. – Chorus:

I was farmin on the shares, and I always was poor,
My crops I took to the farmer's store,
My wife got sick and died on the cabin floor. - Chorus:

Now as I look around, it's mighty plain to see,
This wide and wicked world is a funny place to be,
The gambling man is rich and the workingman is poor. - Chorus:

Chester William "Chet" Powers, Jr. was an American singer-songwriter, and a member of the rock group Quicksilver Messenger Service. He was also known by the stage name "Dino Valenti". (Wikepedia) I met Dino only once in Boston in 1961. He game through town writing, singing contemporary material, and carrying scuba gear. He was off for parts unknown, but was good friends with Karen. Among her repertoire she had 6 songs of Dino's hand printed in large type, arranged and ready to record marked "Side one" and "Side two". And "side three" Also there was an undated early handwritten song of Dino's. They were either from an album of Dino's or were part of an album or single that Karen was going to record solo or they were going to do together at some point. I have not been able to find any other info on these tunes. Here they are:

GENTLE THURSDAY   (Side I)   Dino Valenti

We come to love
We come to laugh
We come to lie in the bosom of this day

Gentle Thursday
Come only once a year
Isn't that a shame
Gentle People
There's no leer
Loving just once a year
Playing that game
It's not the same
If you love me, I'll love you
But you won't let me know you
I can't see how you can keep me from
Falling in love

Don't run – you can't hide
Where could you go, with no one around
Tryin' to bring some truth to this thing
But bringing only gently falling rain

Gentle Thursday
Comes only once a year
Ain't that a shame
If you love me I'll Love you
You promise to be true
Do the things we do
Once a year
I will say hello to you
Tryin' to get to know you
Through the things he way we'll do
things that I will show you
Things you've never seen before
Cause I never showed nobody
We will open other doors
That never have been ready

One day out of the year
Don't run - you can't hide
Where could you go, with no one around
Trying to bring some truth to this thing
But bringing only the gently falling rain

We'll play in the sun
Tryin' to have some fun
Being everyone
Looking down on none
Until Friday comes
We'll be living this life – loving this way
With nothing to hide – jus for one day

Not mind the pain
From sadness refrain
Oh, tomorrow

Gentle Thursday
Love day
Come play
Isn't that a shame

CHILDBIRTH IN THE SUN   (Side II)   Dino Valenti

Let me pull your coat my frien'
The game you play,you'll never win
It's not a game that's played by rules
It's made by man and played by fools
Solitude is what you'll gain
Life is what you lose my friend.

You'd better stop, take a look around
Somebody's gonna see you

You feel like a speeding vine
You laugh to laugh and you end up crying
All the others that you see
Aren't half as real as they could be
You hear 'em sayin' It's all a game
But your wondering if your goin' insane

You'd better stop, take a look around
I'm sure somebody loves you.

Oh come with me – take me – know your mind

Don't weep for those you have left behind
Know as rivers run, you are children of the sun
Look for love and life alone
There's no time to try it on anybody
You go long with what you see
Still you know, you're not free
You say it's cause I'm just one man
But they can't change it – no one man can
Yet it should be plain to see
They are they and we are we
And hasn't anybody told you baby, how much we need you.

You think you can fool them all
You say your life is just a cherry red ball
\And yeah, everything's all right
And nothings got you up tight
Yet a long wakin' night you're lyin'
You think nobody hears you cryin'
That's not the way it is baby -
I always hear you

And when they take the lead you know your mind
Don't weep for those you rob of sleep behind
And know, as roads run -

You are children of the sun
Look for lovin' lifelong
There's no time (be mine) to spend Tryin' on anybody
115
There will be those who'll put you down.
They'll say that you don't know your way around
They'll tell your girl friend that your not a gas
You'll smile and say that cat cat ain't got no class

Maybe they do everything that they can do.
Try to get you thinkin' there's something irradically wrong with you.
You'd better stop – take another look at them,
They have all the problems.

Then come with me - take me

You know your mind
There's no time baby, there's must no time
And you know as rivers run
You are children of the Sunday
Live for all lifelong – don't spend time
Bending your mind
Try and find some way
To own anybody

YOU CAN'T TELL ME (Side II)   Dino Valenti

You can't tell me this ain't my way
Flyin' easy easy but I'm always carin'
When I see you runin' away
Always hidin' and never sharin'
Oh love, how can you do this to me
Turn me round you thin young maiden
Who can tell me I cannot try
Fine answers, cute questions
That's alright if you's rather die
While I'm livin' here I'll be searchin'
Oh my love don't do this to me
Turn my round you thin young - no baby
I just can't let you go down - down
Well, my love can't bring you down
With all your dreams behind you down
Nobody left to remind you, dream

You can;t make me leave you alone
While I love you and you cryin'

All your problems still are my own
As I'm loving you so I'll be tryin'
Oh, my love,, you done things to me
To turn me from your thin young dream

I JUST WANT TO LOVE YOU   Dino Valenti

I don't ever want to see you cryin'
I don't ever want to make you blue

All, all I ever wanted to do is know you
Mean thing, you can know me too.

I don't want to make you sorry
There ain't a a thing you ever said I done, oh, no!
All I ever wanted to do was talk to you
Mean thing you let me be - - - - -

Never spoil your party babe
And tell you where to go and what to do
All I ever wanted to do was love you
Mean thing, you can love me too
Baby I'm in love with you

LOVE SONG   Side (III)   Dino Valenti

Some thoughts you my darling sigh
Kiss her lips where my lips held lies
Kiss her eyes where she'll try to hide
Oh you must touch her softly
I have hurt her so, you must touch her gently

Send her some song to kiss her hair
Say I;ll follow her anywhere
Tell her gently that I care – still care
But you must touch her softly
I have hurt her so - you must touch her gently

Tell her love is all these things]
Gentle sounds two lovers sing
And that true love has reigned as king
But you must tell her softly
For me, for her to know that I will
Love her oh so gently
touch her, lover, gently

STAND BY ME   (Side II)   Dino Valenti

And I bring to you darling all my love
My hand to hold lest you fall my love

There are so many things
Baby that we can do
There are so many ways
I can love you – let me love you
Come and stand by me baby – come stand by me my love.

Those gray clouds make my baby blue
Soon those clouds all will fade from view
There are so many things girl
Yet to be
There are so many ways
I could love you – won't you love me

Please stand by me baby - come stand by me now
Stand by me baby – please stand by me my love.

Summertime girl is sure to come
Oh, summer day bring the summer sun
There are somany things baby that we could do
There are so many ways I could love you
Let me love you

Please stand by me now
Come stand by me baby - come now
Stand now, my love

A PARENTAL PLAN FOR A CHILDHOOD TOMB Tim Hardin
1967
Key of A
In the last sweet moments of a childhood sleep
I gazed briefly on what dream could keep
And then I wished with a childish hope
The dream inside was like a waiting rope
And their to run and climb unafraid
Approach the enchanted play parade

There in the order of ones and threes
Everyone drunk and each dress as they please
The circus of the passing game
Has found my eyes and read my mind

Saying"come if your wish is well
And run away from the schoolhouse bell"

 I held close to sleep and to my dreams
Until I almost joined their passing
And then I awoke and saw the room
A parental plea of a childhood hope
And then I wished with a childhood touch
To dream inside on a waiting rope

WHITE LIES   Tom Danaher 1973

I woke up in a fever
Shaken and humbled by a dream
Believe I might believe in my life
Believe in all life means

Chorus: It's the same white lies
              It's the same old shame
              Its the same white lies
              It's the same damn thing

Got myself up to practice some more
And put all my theories to work
It changed, changed mama it changed
Changed not better, for worse   -   Chorus:

I LOVE YOU MORE THAN WORDS CAN SAY   Eddie Floyd

Please let me sit down beside you
I've got something to tell you darling
I just can't wait, no, not another day
I love you more than words can say (yes I do)

Chorus: Living without you is so painful
               I was tempted to call it a day
              You've got me in your hand
              Why can't you understand
              I love you more than words can say (yes I do)

Release: I get no sleep when I lay there in my bed
          Thoughts of you linger in my head   - Chorus

FRAGMENTS   Bruce Gibson

In the pre-dawn light I begin to see
I sit upright in my bed and feel a sense of need
Although we have never met
We are in love again

Chorus: Fragments are bringing yo to me
         Fragments, moments in between
         Oh, you'll know me, I said you'll know me.,
         Oh yes you'll know me and we'll speak no words

And we will drink long depths, from each others eyes
I won't know your face, I'll know your soul and mind
We will stand alone upon the end of time, and be consumed by love
All else is left behind, fragments of something never seen
Fragments of long forgotten dreams
Oh yes you'll know me, and we will speak no words - Chorus:

Are the moments now or are they yesterday – I know
You've never left and yet you've been away
I get a smile inside, as night begins to bend
Entwined in our embrace, focused with day again
Fragments of ecstasy sublime, fragments of universal time
Oh, you will know, oh yes you'll know me

I SHOULD HAVE TOLD YOU   John M, Morier

I should have told you
I've got to get it down just right
Cause tonight you are leaving for the coast
And most of what I feel inside
I have tried hard to conceal
I should have told you how I feel

Chorus: How could I be so unreal
        I should have told you how I feel
        I should have told you
        I should have told you
        How I feel

Could be you didn't care too much
But your touch is so heavy on my mind
It's hard to do what I'm going through
And I'm aching to reveal
I should have told you how I feel

Release: How could I stand and watch it happening
        Right before my dreaming eyes
        The moment come's and goes
        So quickly I reached so slow
        Why did I even try

In an airport all alone
Now your gone the unsaid words
Still linger on
The unsaid words that burn inside - Chorus:

EVERY STORMY NIGHT   D. Dayer for K Dalton
Sun shines in the morning
Rain shines in the night
When you got no baby
You never feel right

Living that lonely life
It's such a shame
And it"s the lonely ones
Who play those phoney games

Sunshine's in the morning
Rain shines in the night

Ever since you left me
I just can't get it right

I had a lonely life
Before we met
Now after losing you
I've reached the lowest yet

(Musical Bridge)

Sun still shines in the morning
Rain shines in the night
I still watch for you
On every stormy night

LONESOME SERVANT   By: Rick   Danko – The Band
(different lyrics then record)

Goodby to the country home
Goodby to the lady I have known
Farewell to the other side
I best just take it in stride
Unfaithful servant you will learn
To find your place I can see it
In your smile and,
Yes, read it in your face

The memories will linger on the good old days,
They're all gone
Oh lonesome servant, can't you see
That we're still one and the same
Just you and me

NEVER TOO FAR   Tim Hardin (Faithful Virtue; BMI)

Things you say can change your way
Like dark to day – the way you are
From day to day your lie's will play
Till your away – but never too far
Do you feel more like going on
When I say I wasn't wrong
To choose you

Does it ease your heart to say
Tomorrow brings another way to lose you
In my wandering sense of time
I'll try to show enough to rhyme
Your changing line
With my slipping sort of step
I'll try to do much better yet
With what I'll get

COME ON OVER TO MY HOUSE   By: Jimmy Dvis

Come on over to my house
Ain't nobody home but me
I got a lot of loving I can spare
Come on and get them I don't care

I never knew a man could be so sweet
I dream about you when I go to sleep
Come on over to my house baby
Nobody's home but me

HORN OF PLENTY   Elmo Plott, August 1971

   D G D Bmi A D G D A Bmi
Hey there Jonah won't you please give me a ride
My true loves waiting on the other side
I've gone a thousand miles, I'm nearly there
Five hundred miles ain't so many

Chorus : For a turn at the horn of plenty
          Oh, the ways I have loved her are many

Her love has made me a desperate man
She's got me traveling just as hard as I can
I swear to God I won't rest till I'm there
Because of the energy she sends me -   Chorus

I've come a long way and I got a ways to go
It wouldn't be so far if I didn't move so slow
Knowing that I'm moving is what's keeping me alive
With a prayer and my good luck to send me -   Chorus:

THE SLIDE ON MOUNT HUASCAR   Peter Kaufman 1962

'Twas the tenth day of January, 1962
That disaster hit the villages of a valley in Peru,
When th villagers went home that night, all was peace and calm
but death was looking down from icy Mount Hu-as-ca-ran...

     Chorus: The rich and the poor, the young and the old,
              Were buried in that avalanche, so deep and so cold –
oh yes
              The rich and the poor, the young and the old
              Were buried in that avalanche, so deep and so cold.

Up there on the mountain-top, near the burning sun,
Stood a mighty block of ice, weighing many a ton
The mountain side was covered with rocks and mud and snow
While the farmers sat at supper in the valley down below.

Then suddenly that mighty block of ice fell with a roar,
And plunged into the canyon, toward the valley floor,
And as it fell those tons of rock and mud began to slide
And formed an avalanche of death, six miles long and wide.

That forty-foot high wave of mud came rolling down the slope,
For man and children in it's path, there wasn't any hope,

They had no chance to say goodbye or even pray for grace,
The ugly sea of mud rushed in and buried every face.

Now when the slide came to a halt, Three thousand men were dead,
The valley now was silent a black cloud overhead,
No help was necessary, 'cos there was none to save,
The young and the old, the rich and poor, lay buried in that grave.

In that lonesome valley, there's no life anymore,
There's no one to rebuild it, or to rebuild it for;
Why those three thousand had to die, no one will ever know,
But out of all that mud and snow, a flowers sure to grow.

DARLING COMPANION   By: June Carter and Johnny Cash

Darling companion come on and give me understanding
And let me be your champion, a hand to hold
Your pretty hand in

Darling companion, now you know
You'll never be abandoned,
love will always shine
On your hand in mine
I can depend on you
Darling companion heaven knows

Where we'll be standing
Just as long as we keep laughing
Keep in mind just what is happening

Darling companion, I'll tell the mountains,
And the Canyons, as long as I've got legs
To stand I'm gonna run to you

A steed like you should have a mare
Down with me is what you need

IF I HAD THE COURAGE (I'D TELL YOU) - Fodoro Music   1969

If I had the courage I'd tell you,
To get out now
Cause I know you'll have to pay
And it don't look easiest anyway

   Chorus: Your the last of the friends I have
            All the rest have gone away, oh no

Started all one Saturday
Should have said what I had to say
I was free to let you know
But I didn't have the courage to let you go - Chorus:

If it's that unusual, then hitchhike home
And your house will be good
Hand around and you'll regret whatever
We had you had better forget - Chorus:

I CANT MAKE IT ANYMORE   Richie Havens – Gordon Lightfoot

I got too low with no reason
You say it's the moon or the season
But somethings changed
And I can't make my mind believe

Baby somethings Wrong
All the feeling;s gone
I can't make it anymore

I don't have the reason why
But I just can't lie
When I feel this way
There are things that I must say

I can't make it anymore
I can't make it anymore

Lately I don't feel much like talking
Stead of going home I just go out walking

And drinking too much
And longing for your touch
Somethings changed, I just don't feel the same

I can't make it anymore
I can't make it anymore

Where did we go wrong?
Where do I belong?
Let me find out when it all began

GOING BACK HOME TO MY DAD   Jimmy Rodgers

I'm dreaming tonight of an old southern town
I've grown so weary of roaming around
I'm going back home to my dad

Chorus: Your hair has turned to silver
    Your cheeks are fading too
     Daddy, dear old Daddy,
     I'm coming home to you

You made my boyhood happy
Still I longed to roam, I've had my way but now I'll say
I long for you and home. - Chorus:

Dear Daddy you shared my sorrows and joys
You tried to bring me up right
Still I just wanted to be just one of the boys
But I'm starting back home tonight. Chorus:

BLACK EYED SUZIE   Justin Townes Earle

WHEN A MAN LOVES A WOMAN Percy Sledge

GREEN DOOR   Bob Davie & Marvin Moore

WHISPERING PINES   R. Robertson & Art Manuel

CAUTIOUSLY   Morey Hayden – Calle Music – ASCAP

GLOOMY SUNDAY
("Gloomy Sunday") is a song composed by Hungarian Pianist and composer
Rezso Seress and pubolished in 1933, as "Vege A vilagnak" ("End of the
World") Lyrics were written by Laszlo Javor, and in his version the song
was retitled "Szomoru vasarnap" (Hungarian pronunciation: 'somore:
'vjoja:mop) ("Sad Sunday"). The song was first recorded in Hungarian by Pal
Kalma in 1935.

"Gloomy Sunday" was first recorded in English by Hal Kemlin in 1936, with
lyrics by Sam M. Lewis, and was recorded the same year by Paul
Roberson, with lyrics by Desmond Carter. It became well known
throughout much ofthe English speaking world after the release of a
version by Billie Holiday in]1941. Lewis's lyrics referred to suicide,
and the record label described it as
the "Hungarian Suicide Song". There is a recurring urban legend that
claimsthat many people committed suicide with this song playing.
(Wikepedia)

KATIE MAY   Grateful Dead

LAND OF LOVE   Richard Goslin

I WOULD BE TRUE   Hymn: Howard A. Walter (1883-1918)

SWEET SUBSTITUTE   Jelly Roll Morton – 1941

WHO BUILT THE WALL   Keith Stoner & Mickey Stoner

MY BABY MUST BE A MAGICIAN William Robinson – Motor
Record Corp.

FIXING A HOLE   J. Lennon & P. McCartney

JUST AS BLUE AS I CAN BE   Jimmy Rogers

OTHER SIDE OF THIS LIFE   Fred Neil

CAN'T BUY ME LOVE   Beatles

MEMPHIS   Chuck Berry

FINE WAY TO GO   Lonnie Mack 1971

THE STRANGER   Jerry Merrick

THEY'LL BE PEACE IN THE VALLEY FOR ME Tomas A. Dorsey

YOU'VE GOT A FRIEND   Carole King

KINGDOM IN HEAVEN   Paul Caruso

I NEVER KNEW WHAT A KISS COULD BE – Beatles

REACH OUT FOR ME   Dion Warwick

THESE ARE NOT MY PEOPLE   Joe South

MANY A TEAR HAS TO FALL   Dawes & Sigman

BABY'S GOOD TO ME   Beatles

TOM JOAD   Woody Guthrie

IT'S A LONG WAY HOME   Jerry Merric

SONG LISTS AND GIG SHEETS

There are 9 lists. Some are lists for album tracks, others are list for gigs, and some are notes for her own repertoire. Clues as to what she was into when, as she matured as an artist, can be found here.
They are presented in as close to chronological order as I can discern.
(P.W.)

1) Blind Man -

    Cotton Fields - (Capo 2nd fret, C tuning)

    Ain't No Grave -   (Capo 2nd fret, C tuning)

    Circle Be Unbroken   - (Capo 4nd fret, C tuning)

    Black Girlfriend -   (Capo 2nd fret, C tuning)

    Moonshine   - (D guitar in D G - Banjo in C)

    Sweet William Died -

    No More   -

    What You Gonna Do?   -

    East Colorado Banjo (Banjo D G G ((4 5 3)

    All My Trials

    (12 string tuned D G C F A D ((6 5 4 3 2 1))
    (6 string tuned C F B E G C ((6 5 4 3 2 1))
    (banjo D B D G B ((4 3 2 1 5))

2) Blues on My Ceiling   C A7 D F A

Just a Little Bit of Rain   D

Right Wrong Or Ready

More Than Words Can Say

Ribbon Bow

Sweet Substitute

Dino's Song   C Dmi F C (2) Dmi (2) F (2) G (2)

Down on the Street   G   (Fannin Stereet)

Broonzy Blues

Turn the Page

More Than Words   -   release: A G E F# A B E

Ribbon Bow   -   Emi A F# G (3) A F#mi Emi

Right Wrong or Ready - G#mi F#mi A Bmi E Bmi F#mi A

3)   Same Old Man   Steve Weber

        Turn the Page   Hardin

        Don't Listen to Me   Havens

        Traveling Shoes   Neil

        Ain't Had No Loving   Tucker

        Memphis   Barry?

        Badi Da   Neil

        Bourgeois   Leadbelly

Dock of The Day	??	
Echoes	Neil	
When the Sun Shines	Tucker	
Walk With Me	Tucker	
Maggie's Farm	Dylan	
Good Morning Blues	Traditional	
Don't Make Promises	Hardin	
I Can't Make it Anymore	Havens/Lightfoot	
Leaving in The Morning	Traditional	
Sweet Mama	Neil	

4)

Walk With Me Baby	E
Dolphin In The Sea	E
Darling Companion	C
Same Old Man	D
Hank Williams	G
Sweet Mama	E
3 Day Eternity	C
Maggie's Farm	A
High Flying Bird	Ami
Can't Make It Anymore	E

Before I met you	G
Can't tell a book	E
Oh, Lord You Know	A
Another Side Of This Life	G
Memphis	E
Don't Make Promises	E
Blues On My Ceiling	
Ain't It A Shame	
Sweet Mama	
When I Get Home	
Ben DuBarry	
Beale Street Blues	
Hoboin	
Fixin To Die	

5) Feeding My Sheep

Can't Make it Anymore

My Home's Across (The River)

Fannin Street

Cotton Eyed Joe

Ben DuBarry

Lonesome Valley

Sweet Whatdoyoucallit

Sweet William

Yellow is The Color

Maggie's Farm

Morning Blues

6) Trouble in Mind   Picture

Crawdad Song   God Bless The Child

Cool Colorado   Sowing on The Mountain

Someday Sweetheart   In the Evening

Ribbon Bow   Viper

Cocaine   Wine Spodi Oh Di

Across the Blue Ridge   When first Unto (This Country)

Feed My Sheep   Green (Rocky Road)

Rising Sun   One May

Mississippi River   Mole

2:19 (Blues)   East Virginia

Rampart Street   Nottingham

Easy Rider   Katy Cruel

Honky Tonk Tavern   Lonesome Valley

You Don't Know	Sweet William
Cotton Eyed Joe	Whopee Ligio
Oh, Freedom	Fannin Street
7) Black is he Color	Oh Shenandoah
Look Where That Road Grow High	Let The Grass
Mountain Hymn Chariot	Greetings to the
Observations of The Mecurial Looking Glass	Out Through the
Orpheus and The Sound of Awakening Apprentice	Song of The
Song of the Wanderer	Utopia Street Cafe
This Road Has No Beginning	Not Enough of You
Song to Anyone	No More
Talking Woodstock	Sing Sweet Harp
Long Way Down	Runaway
Nobody's Fault But My Own	Broken Wing
Lion in Love	Talking Babylon Shock
Goodbye is a Lonely Song	
8) K. D. Cruel	
Right Wrong or Ready	

Leaving For The Country

Too Late To Say You're Mine

Little Bit of Rain

How Sweet It Is

Waiting For The Sun

Same Old Man

Nickel and Dime

One Night of Love   E C F G F G A

Something on Your Mind

In My Own Dream

Blues On My Ceiling

More Than Words

Shiloh

Traveling Shoes

Cry For Me (Down on the Street)

9) (21 Songs)

Blues in A (When Things Go Wrong, or In The Evening)

Turn The Page	Reefer
Traveling Shoes	Cotton
Right Wrong or Ready	Down on The Street

While Your On Your Way

Sweet S.

Oh, Freedom

Rocky Road

God Bless The Child

Rain

Something On Your Mind

Blues Colorado

Blues on My Ceiling

Blues in E (2:19)

Ribbon Bow

Katy Cruel or Some Old Man

More Than Words Can Say

Follow

Remembering Mountains (K. D.)

INDEX OF SONGS (AND POEMS) (ALPHABETICAL)

These are the songs that Karen performed, collected, or wrote with the intention of "Stylizing" and Recording/Performing them. They represent the best of America's Music, and the fusion of cultures and sources that make up "American Music". I think that in this collection of songs, she has come very close to defining what that is.

"Into the dark or the blinding light, either way you can't see a thing"
K.D.

(December 1992)

www.ingramcontent.com/pod-product-compliance
Lightning Source LLC
LaVergne TN
LVHW081333060426
835513LV00014B/1268